Communications in Computer and Information Science 591

Commenced Publication in 2007
Founding and Former Series Editors:
Alfredo Cuzzocrea, Dominik Ślęzak, and Xiaokang Yang

Editorial Board

More information about this series at http://www.springer.com/series/7899

Florian Daniel · Cesare Pautasso (Eds.)

Rapid Mashup Development Tools

First International Rapid Mashup Challenge, RMC 2015
Rotterdam, The Netherlands, June 23, 2015
Revised Selected Papers

Springer

Editors
Florian Daniel
DISI/RP SI
University of Trento
Povo, Trento
Italy

Cesare Pautasso
University of Lugano
Lugano
Switzerland

ISSN 1865-0929   ISSN 1865-0937 (electronic)
Communications in Computer and Information Science
ISBN 978-3-319-28726-3   ISBN 978-3-319-28727-0 (eBook)
DOI 10.1007/978-3-319-28727-0

Library of Congress Control Number: 2015959582

Printed on acid-free paper

This Springer imprint is published by SpringerNature
The registered company is Springer International Publishing AG Switzerland

Preface

This volume prints the proceedings of the ICWE 2015 Rapid Mashup Challenge (http://mashup.inf.usi.ch/challenge/2015/) that was held on June 23, 2015, in Rotterdam, The Netherlands, in conjunction with the 15th International Conference on Web Engineering (ICWE, http://icwe2015.webengineering.org/). The 2015 edition of the challenge is the first installment of a series of challenges that aim to engage researchers and practitioners in a competition for the best mashup approach. The next edition will be held at ICWE 2016 in Lugano, Switzerland.

The contributions contained in this volume are post-challenge extensions of initial, short-version proposals that served for the authors to express their interest to participate in the challenge with little effort and for the organizers of the challenge to select participants based on the interestingness and maturity of the proposals. The short versions of the contributions are available online in the program section of the challenge: http://mashup.inf.usi.ch/challenge/2015/program.html.

We would like to thank the authors for their excellent work before and after the challenge as well as for their commitment and engagement during the challenge itself. The presented tools and approaches are of course the core of the event and of this volume. We would also like to thank the jury that helped rate contributions and assure quality in the post-challenge preparation of the contributions printed in this volume. Of course, we would like to thank Springer, especially Aliaksandr Birukou, for promoting and publishing the proceedings of the challenge in their CCIS series, a choice that allowed us to provide a complete picture of the proposals the challenge attracted, without having to be too strict on the acceptance of contributions in the first place and allowing us to work together with the authors on their contributions in the post-challenge phase.

We are grateful to everyone who contributed to this volume and confident the reader will find the content interesting, inspiring, and – hopefully – also challenging.

September 2015

Florian Daniel
Cesare Pautasso

Jury Members

Contents

ICWE 2015 Rapid Mashup Challenge: Introduction

Florian Daniel[1(✉)] and Cesare Pautasso[2]

[1] University of Trento, Via Sommarive 9, 38123 Povo, TN, Italy
`daniel@disi.unitn.it`
[2] Faculty of Informatics, University of Lugano (USI), Lugano, Switzerland
`cesare.pautasso@usi.ch`

Abstract. The ICWE 2015 Rapid Mashup Challenge is the first installment of a series of challenges that aim to engage researchers and practitioners in a competition for the best mashup approach. This paper
introduces the reader to the general context of the Challenge, its objec-
tives and motivation. It summarizes its structure into phases and the
requirements contributions were asked to satisfy, so as to be eligible for
participation. A brief summary of the contributions that were selected
for presentation provides an overview of the content of the remainder of
this volume.

Keywords: Mashups · Mashup tools · Challenge · Benchmarking

1 Context and Objective

By now, it's more or less a decade that the scientific community and industry
use the term "mashup" in the context of Web engineering to refer to a type of
Web application that heavily relies on the reuse of third-party constituent elements in their development. In fact, we usually define a mashup as "a composite
application developed starting from reusable data, application logic and/or user
interfaces typically, but not mandatorily, sourced from the Web" [1]. Mashups
have been associated with their situational nature and the serendipitous reuse of
components not necessarily originally intended for the purpose of the mashup.
That is, the term mashup refers more to the way applications are developed and
less to a specific type of application as perceived by its users – in the end we are
always talking about a Web application.

The ICWE 2015 Rapid Mashup Challenge (the Challenge, http://mashup.
inf.usi.ch/challenge/2015) acknowledges this peculiarity of mashups and puts its
focus on the techniques, approaches, libraries, and tools that researchers and
practitioners have come up with so far to aid the development of mashups.
This perspective is different from the perspectives of similar challenges known
from other contexts or communities. For instance, the Semantic Web Challenge
(http://challenge.semanticweb.org/) focuses on the application of Semantic Web
[2] technologies in the development of software with commercial potential, large

© Springer International Publishing Switzerland 2016
F. Daniel and C. Pautasso (Eds.): RMC 2015, CCIS 591, pp. 1–11, 2016.
DOI: 10.1007/978-3-319-28727-0_1

user bases, or functionality that is useful and of societal value. The AI Mashup Challenge (http://aimashup.org/), instead, more specifically focuses on mashups that use AI (Artificial Intelligence) technology (e.g., machine learning and data mining, machine vision, natural language processing, reasoning, ontologies) and intelligence to mashup existing resources. The ICWE 2015 Rapid Mashup Challenge does not limit its focus to any specific technology and rather aims to compare how mashups are developed, independently of how their internals look like.

The maturity and sophistication of mashup tools/approaches has been growing over the past decade. Many research projects and industry tools have been dedicated to design and develop tools for the composition of Web services, Web data sources and Web widgets. Given their diversity, comparing and evaluating mashup approaches has been very challenging. Doing so from a practice-oriented point of view is the goal of the Challenge, of course, while still keeping also an eye on the quality and usefulness of the mashups developed during the Challenge. The only constraints we introduced concerned the required use of a set of representative Web APIs and the strict time limit of 10 min for the construction of the mashup itself.

In the following, we describe all the pre-challenge aspects, such as the Call for Participation, the requirements candidate approaches had to satisfy, the organization of the Challenge itself, as well as the set of selected competitors. The following articles in this volume describe each of the contributions individually and report on the mashups developed live during the Challenge using these tools. The last article in this volume then provides insight into the voting procedure and tool and the outcomes of the Challenge, including the winner.

2   Participation Requirements and Organization

2.1   Call for Participation and Requirements

In line with the above goals of the Challenge, this year's call for participation started as follows:

> The ICWE 2015 Rapid Mashup Challenge launches a competition between mashup approaches/tools with special attention to their expressiveness and speed. We invite developers and researchers working on mashups, mashup tools and assisting technologies to compete in the creation of the most interesting and/or complex mashup they can develop within a given time boundary, using a given set of source components. The goal of the Challenge is to allow everybody working on mashups and composite Web applications to showcase their ideas and solutions and to establish an event that is both challenging and fun.
>
> We are interested in all kinds of mashup composition tools and approaches: from programming languages, domain-specific languages to natural language, from visual modeling tools to textual ones, etc. Submissions will be screened based on relevance, originality and maturity. Admitted contributions will be evaluated as follows: Points will be given

by a jury for the complexity of the resulting mashup, the elegance of its construction and the features of the mashup tool/approach that have been used to build it. The public will also be able to give feedback and participate in the challenge evaluation process.

The call highlights the three key aspects of the evaluation:

- *Complexity of mashup*: The key criterion of any development environment is of course the quality of the output it is able to generate. In the case of mashup tools/approaches, this output are the mashups. During the Challenge, participants were therefore asked to showcase live the development of a mashup using their own tool/approach, whose complexity and quality as application was assessed.
- *Elegance of construction*: Talking about aiding the development of software, it is important to look at how this aid is implemented. The elegance of construction, in this respect, refers to how easy the proposed mashup tool/approach is perceived, how efficient the jury and audience think the tool is compared to the state of the art, and which benefits it provides to its users.
- *Features of mashup approach*: Finally, since a single mashup may not be able to showcase all the features of a proposed tool/approach, it is also good to have a look at which exact development features it provides. For instance, a tool that is oriented toward professional programmers is fundamentally different from one that instead targets end-users.

As for the kind of mashup tool/approach that was considered eligible to participate, the Challenge was very open, and all kinds of mashup composition tools and approaches were allowed: from programming languages, domain-specific languages to natural language and visual modeling tools. The limitation was only the imagination and creativity of the participants. The complexity of mashups and the features of the mashup tool/approach were self-declared by the authors using a dedicated feature checklist (see Sect. 3) and assessed by the jury and the audience during the Challenge.

2.2   Structure of Challenge

The Challenge was organized into four phases:

1. *Admission*: Submission of application. The application should include a brief description of the proposed tool/approach and a filled feature checklist.
2. *Preparation*: If a proposal was accepted to the challenge, the authors received a list of Web APIs that are allowed to be used to compose the demo mashup during the competition. This preparation phase gave the authors about one month to prepare for the event.
3. *Competition*: During the ICWE conference, participants had to give a live demonstration of how you build their own mashup within at most 10 min of time, preceded by a 10–15 minutes presentation of their approach and preparation for the Challenge. The time limits made the challenge more challenging.

4. *Post-challenge*: Preparation of post-challenge paper explaining the proposed solution and giving technical details about the approach and how it was used to rapidly build the mashup.

The goal of this structure was to have authors focus more on the practical aspects before the Challenge (the preparation of their demonstration), while asking them to concentrate on the conceptual and scientific aspects afterwards (with the writing of the paper to be included in the proceedings). Submitted applications for participation were evaluated by the organizers of the Challenge based on the relevance and maturity of the proposed approach.

3   Feature Checklist

In order to facilitate the comparison of approaches, authors were required to accompany their submission with a filled feature checklist that describes the two key parts of the evaluation, i.e., the nature of the mashups that their tool/approach allows one to develop and the development features of the proposed tool. Figure 1 graphically summarizes the features identified as relevant for the Challenge, while the following subsections describe the features in more detail.

3.1   Mashup Features

In order to be able to compare the mashups produced by the different approaches during the Challenge, the mashup features proposed by Daniel and Matera [1] were taken as reference:

- **Mashup type:** The mashup type expresses the positioning of the mashup at one or more of the three layers of the typical application stack (data, logic, presentation), depending on where the mashup's integration logic is positioned. *Data mashups* operate at the data layer, integrate data sources, and are typically published again as data sources (e.g., RSS feeds or RESTful Web services). *Logic mashups* integrate components at the application logic layer, reuse data and application logic (e.g., Web services), and are typically published as Web services. *User Interface (UI) mashups* are located at the presentation layer, integrate UI components/widgets, and are published as Web applications that users can interact with via the Web browser. Finally, *hybrid mashups* span multiple layers of the application stack.
- **Component types:** The types of mashups introduced above strongly relate to the types of the components they integrate. *Data components* comprise RSS and Atom feeds, XML JSON, CSV and similar data resources, web data extractions, micro-formats, but also SOAP or RESTful web services that are used as data services only. *Logic components* comprise SOAP and RESTful web services, JavaScript APIs and libraries, device APIs, and API extractions. *UI components* comprise code snippets and JavaScript UI libraries, Java portlets, widgets and gadgets, web clips and extracted UI components.

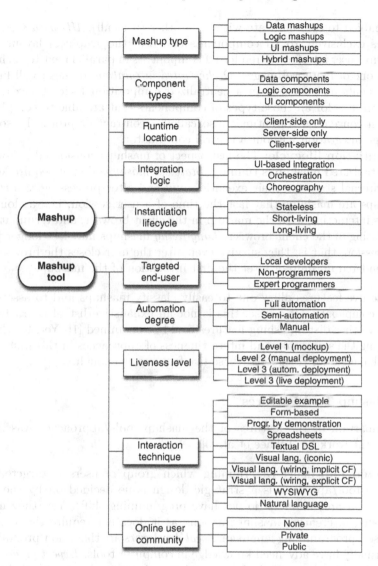

Fig. 1. The feature checklist used to compare and position mashup approaches.

– **Runtime location:** There are generally a variety of possible architectural configurations that may be adopted for the development of mashups, compatibly with the requirements of the chosen components. *Client-side* mashups are executed in the client browser. *Server-side* mashups are executed in the server. *Client-server* mashups are distributed over client and server, and both parts interact the one with the other at runtime.
– **Integration logic:** The integration logic tells how integration happens, that is, how components are used to form a composite application and how they

are enabled to communicate with each other (if at all). *UI-based integration* applies exclusively to UI components and uses the graphical layout of the mashup's user interface to render UI components in parallel next to each other inside one or more web pages. *Orchestrated integration* applies to all kinds of components and consists in a centralized composition logic. *Choreographed integration* is for all those types of components that are able to comply with a given convention (oftentimes also called a contract or protocol), so as to manage integration without a central coordinator.

– **Instantiation lifecycle:** The last aspect of mashups considered is how long an instantiated mashup is running. *Stateless mashups* do not require keeping any internal state for their execution and end after processing. *Short-living* mashups are mashups that last the time of a user session, i.e., as long as a user is interacting with the mashup in the client browser, and terminate with the closing of the client browser. *Long-living* mashups may last longer than a user session, that is, they survive even after the user closes the browser with the rendered mashup or after the first invocation of the mashup.

These five features allow one to easily classify mashups and to assess their internal complexity. Of course, this is not an exhaustive list of characteristics and many other distinguishing features could be examined [1]. Yet, for the sake of assessing the suitability and interestingness of approaches in this first version of the Challenge we considered these five features as enough.

3.2 Mashup Tool Features

The comparison of the features of the mashup tools/approaches was instead based on the work by Aghaee et al. [3].

– **Targeted end-user:** Determining which group of users is targeted by a mashup tool/approach is a strategic design issue decided on by the developers. *Non-programmers* do not have programming skills. Yet, they may be interested in creating mashups as long as it does not require them to learn and use a programming language. *Local developers* are those non-programmers who usually have advanced knowledge in computer tools. *Expert programmers* have adequate programming skills and experience to develop mashups using programming and scripting languages (e.g., JavaScript and PHP).

– **Automation degree:** The automation degree of a mashup tool refers to how much of the development process can be undertaken by the tool on behalf of its users. *Full automation* of mashup development eliminates the need for direct involvement of users in the development process. *Semi-automatic* tools partially automate mashup development by providing guidance and assistance. *Manual* approaches do not provide any automated support during development; typically, these approaches come in the form of programming libraries or runtime middlewares.

– **Liveness level:** Tanimoto proposed the concept of liveness [4], according to which four levels of liveness can be distinguished. At *Level 1* (non-executable prototype mockup), a tool is just used to create prototype mashups that are not directly connected to any kind of run-time system. *Level 2* (explicit compilation and deployment steps) of liveness is characterized by mashup design blueprints that carry sufficient details to give them an executable semantics. *Level 3* (automatic compilation and deployment) tools support rapid deployment into operation, e.g., triggered by each edit-change or by an explicit action executed by the developer. *Level 4* (dynamic modification of running mashup) of mashup liveness is obtained by the tools that support live modification of the mashup code, while it is being executed.

– **Interaction technique:** There have been a number of interaction techniques through the use of which the barriers of programming can be lifted to its developers [5]. *Editable examples* let users modify and change the behavior of existing examples, instead of programming from scratch. In *form-based* interaction, users are asked to fill out a form to create a new or change the behavior of an existing object. *Programming by demonstration* suggests to teach a computer by example how to accomplish a particular task. *Spreadsheets* are one of the most popular and widely used end-user programming approaches to store, manipulate, and display complex data. *Textual DSLs* are languages targeted to address specific problems in a particular domain; they have a textual syntax that may or may not resemble an existing general-purpose programming language. A *visual language* (iconic), as opposed to a textual programming language, is any programming language that uses visual symbols, syntax, and semantics. Some visual languages support *wiring with implicit control flow*, where the control flow of the mashup is derived from its data flow graph. Other visual languages support *wiring with explicit control flow*, where the control flow is explicitly defined, for instance, by adding directed arrows connecting the boxes, or putting the boxes in a specific order (e.g., from left to right). *WYSIWYG* (What You See Is What You Get) enables users to create and modify a mashup on a graphical user interface that is similar to the one that will appear when the mashup runs. *Natural language* allows developers to express their mashup via a restricted, controlled set of natural language constructs (e.g., a subset of English) that can be interpreted unequivocally by a runtime environment.

– **Online user community:** Online communities are an important resource in assisting developers, especially end-users, to program [6]. If a tool does not support any online community (*none*), it is harder to leverage on the experience of others. In *public* communities, the content is accessible to any user on the Web who wishes to join the community (with or without registration). In *private* communities, the authority to join the community is granted on the basis of compliance with some operator-specified criteria.

Like for the mashup features, also in the case of the mashup tools/approaches many other characteristics could be considered (e.g., collaboration). The features selected for the Challenge, however, already provide good insight into the philosophy behind each approach, and we preferred to keep the list concise.

4   Participants

The purpose of the above feature checklist with its 10 features is threefold: firstly, it allows interested participants to understand what kind of contributions the Challenge is interested in; secondly, it allows the organizers of the Challenge to pre-screen contributions and select submissions for inclusion in the Challenge and proceedings; and, thirdly, it allows the participants to better position their contributions and the jury and audience to better compare the contributions. The first two steps led to the following list of participants to the ICWE 2015 Rapid Mashup Challenge (we postpone the discussion of the jury/audience assessment to the concluding article of this volume):

- **FlexMash**: Extended Techniques for Flexible Modeling and Execution of Data Mashups, by Pascal Hirmer and Bernhard Mitschang. FlexMash is a visual mashup tool for the development of data mashups that targets non-programmers. The tools pays particular attention to flexibility and extensibility to enable the integration of heterogeneous data sources as well as the dynamic (un-)tethering of data sources. The authors participate with a prototypical implementation of their tool.
- **UI-Oriented Computing**: Interactive, Live Mashup Development through UI-Oriented Computing, by Anis Nouri and Florian Daniel. UI-oriented computing is less an individual mashup tool and more a novel idea of programming paradigm that looks at the Surface Web as at a programming environment and aims to support interactive and live mashup development inside the Web browser, without requiring users to program any line of code. The authors participate in the Challenge with a prototype implementation of a Web browser extensions that extends the browser with UI-oriented computing capabilities.
- **SmartComposition**: Extending Web Applications to Multi-Screen Mashups, by Michael Krug, Fabian Wiedemann and Martin Gaedke. SmartComposition takes mashups to a different level by proposing an environment based on Web components that supports the development of multi-screen mashups, that is, mashups that are naturally distributed over multiple devices. Web sockets allow the environment to synchronize components across screens. The authors participate with a prototype environment with support for dynamic runtime modifications.
- **EFESTO**: A platform for the End-User Development of Interactive Workspaces for Data Exploration, by Giuseppe Desolda, Carmelo Ardito and Maristella Matera. EFESTO is a platform for the creation of interactive workspaces supporting end-users in the exploration and seamless composition of heterogeneous data sources. Internally, it makes use of Linked Open Data, so as to provide its users with advanced data integration features almost for free. The authors showcase their current implementation of development environment in the form of a workspace for integrating UI components and data sources.
- **WebMakeup**: Empowering Users to Mod Websites, by Oscar Diaz, Iñigo Aldalur, Cristobal Arellano, Haritz Medina and Sergio Firmenich. Also WebMakeup proposes an original perspective on the problem of mashup development: instead of proposing an own, new development environment, it leverages

Table 1. Overview of the mashup and mashup tool features declared by the approaches that participated in the ICWE 2015 Rapid Mashup Challenge.

			FlexMash	UI-Oriented Computing	Smart-Composition	EFESTO	WebMakeup	WLS
Mashup	Mashup type	Data mashups	✓					
		Logic mashups						✓
		UI mashups			✓		✓	
		Hybrid mashups		✓	✓	✓		
	Component types	Data components	✓		✓	✓		
		Logic components			✓	✓		✓
		UI components		✓	✓	✓	✓	
	Runtime location	Client-side only			✓		✓	
		Server-side only						
		Client-server	✓		✓	✓		✓
	Integration logic	UI-based integr.		✓		✓	✓	
		Orchestration	✓			✓		
		Choreography			✓			✓
	Instantiation lifecycle	Stateless	✓					
		Short-living		✓	✓	✓	✓	✓
		Long-living				✓		
Mashup tool	Target end-user	Local developers			✓			
		Non-programmers	✓	✓		✓	✓	
		Expert programmers		✓				✓
	Automation degree	Full automation						
		Semi-automation	✓	✓		✓	✓	✓
		Manual		✓	✓			
	Liveness level	Level 1 (mockup)						
		Level 2 (manual)						
		Level 3 (automatic)	✓				✓	
		Level 4 (dynamic)		✓	✓	✓		✓
	Interaction technique	Editable examples			✓			
		Form-based						
		Progr. by demonstration		✓				
		Spreadsheets						
		Textual DSL		✓				✓
		Visual (iconic)	✓					
		Visual (wiring, implicit)				✓		
		Visual (wiring, explicit)						
		WYSIWYG		✓			✓	
		Natural language						
	Online user community	None	✓	✓	✓	✓		✓
		Private					✓	
		Public						

on the Web browser and the applications running therein as natural environment for the modding (client-side extension) of existing applications (e.g., by adding widgets that fetch data from other applications). The authors participate with their publicly available Chrome extension.

- **WLS**: Mashup Development with Web Liquid Streams, by Masiar Babazadeh, Andrea Gallidabino and Cesare Pautasso. Finally, Web Liquid Streams (WLS) delves into one peculiar aspects of modern mashups, i.e., streaming data. The approach enables the development of mashups with streaming operators that support the live, runtime integration of data streams. The authors showcase the use of their dynamic streaming framework that takes advantage of standard Web protocols and targets expert programmers.

Table 1 summarizes the characteristics of the selected approaches as declared by the authors. Compared to the emergence of mashups, the approaches represent well the recent focus of the mashup community on the user interface side of mashups. In fact, UI mashups are widely considered most suitable for end-users without programming skills, and end-users have been in the mind of mashup tool developers from the very beginning on. Thanks to the availability of stable JavaScript communication technologies, such as AJAX, it is also evident, that more and more approaches enable the development of full-fledged, client-server mashups whose resource consumption can strategically be distributed over client (e.g., for UI synchronization) and server (e.g., for data integration). Interestingly, most of the proposed approaches feature mashups with a short-lived lifecycle, that is, mashups that run inside the Web browser as long as the browser is open.

On the development support side, a preference for dynamic, live development approaches (level 4) is evident – again, in line with the latest trends in end-user development. The paradigms proposed to approach development (the interaction techniques) are, instead, very heterogeneous and led to a very varied and diversified live demo session during the Challenge. The degree of automation is mostly that of semi-automation, while only one tool (WebMakeup) already has an own online user community. This last result is strictly related with the early stage of development (prototypes) of most of the proposed approaches.

We believe the selected mashup approaches represent a vivid and cutting-edge picture of the state of the art in research on mashups development and are confident the reader will enjoy discovering how each tool was able to compete in the challenge, as described in the next chapters.

References

1. Daniel, F., Matera, M.: Mashups: Concepts, Models and Architectures. Springer, Heidelberg (2014)
2. Berners-Lee, T., Hendler, J., Lassila, O.: The semantic web. Sci. Am. **284**(5), 34–43 (2001)
3. Aghaee, S., Nowak, M., Pautasso, C.: Reusable decision space for mashup tool design. In: Barbosa, S.D.J., Campos, J.C., Kazman, R., Palanque, P.A., Harrison, M.D., Reeves, S. (eds.) EICS, pp. 211–220. ACM (2012)
4. Tanimoto, S.L.: VIVA: a visual language for image processing. J. Vis. Lang. Comput. **1**(2), 127–139 (1990)

5. Myers, B.A., Ko, A.J., Burnett, M.M.: Invited research overview: end-user programming. In: CHI 2006 Extended Abstracts on Human Factors in Computing Systems,
pp. 75–80. ACM (2006)
6. Nardi, B.A.: A Small Matter of Programming: Perspectives on End User Computing.
MIT Press, Cambridge (1993)

FlexMash – Flexible Data Mashups Based on Pattern-Based Model Transformation

Pascal Hirmer[✉] and Bernhard Mitschang

Institute of Parallel and Distributed Systems, University of Stuttgart,
Universitätsstr. 38, 70569 Stuttgart, Germany
pascal.hirmer@ipvs.uni-stuttgart.de
http://www.ipvs.uni-stuttgart.de

Abstract. Today, the ad-hoc processing and integration of data is an important issue due to fast growing IT systems and an increased connectivity of the corresponding data sources. The overall goal is deriving high-level information based on a huge amount of low-level data. However, an increasing amount of data leads to high complexity and many technical challenges. Especially non-IT expert users are overburdened with highly complex solutions such as Extract-Transform-Load processes. To tackle these issues, we need a means to abstract from technical details and provide a flexible execution of data processing and integration scenarios. In this paper, we present an approach for modeling and pattern-based execution of data mashups based on Mashup Plans, a domain-specific mashup model that has been introduced in previous work. This non-executable model can be mapped onto different executable ones depending on the use case scenario. The concepts introduced in this paper were presented during the Rapid Mashup Challenge at the International Conference on Web Engineering 2015. This paper presents our approach, the scenario that was implemented for this challenge, as well as the encountered issues during its preparation.

Keywords: ICWE rapid mashup challenge 2015 · Data mashups · Transformation patterns · TOSCA · Cloud computing

1 Context and Goals

Nowadays, the complexity and size of the IT systems used in enterprises constantly increase. Especially in the area of data processing and integration, this leads to high costs as well as communication effort between domain-specific users, e.g., business persons, and IT experts that implement the data processing. This oftentimes results in hand-made, monolithic, non-flexible solutions that are exclusively suitable for a few number of use cases. For example, Extract-Transform-Load (ETL) process models and their execution can usually only be used for specific scenarios, i.e., they offer nearly no flexibility. Furthermore, existing data mashup or data streaming solutions mostly offer a single possibility how data is processed, fulfilling only a limited number of user requirements.

© Springer International Publishing Switzerland 2016
F. Daniel and C. Pautasso (Eds.): RMC 2015, CCIS 591, pp. 12–30, 2016.
DOI: 10.1007/978-3-319-28727-0_2

To tackle these issues, we need a data mashup solution that offers domain-specific modeling as well as a corresponding technical execution of data processing and integration depending on the use case scenario. That is, its execution has to flexibly suite a scenario's special requirements, e.g., robustness, scalability, security, efficiency. Using a non-technical, domain-specific model enables users to define data processing and integration scenarios they are interested in without any need of implementation and execution details. Aside the domain-specific model, the user should have the possibility to define requirements that are fulfilled by the mashup execution. In previous work, we introduced *Mashup Plans* [11], a graph-based model that enables domain-specific modeling of data mashups. Mashup Plans enable modeling data sources as so called *business objects* [6,14] that represent domain-specific objects, e.g., an enterprise information system or a production machine, and abstract from low-level data structures such as databases, ontologies, sensors or unstructured text. In the context of this paper as well as of previous work, these business objects are called *Data Source Descriptions (DSD)*. Furthermore, Mashup Plans contain *Data Processing Descriptions (DPD)* that abstract from fine-grained data operations and offer generic, easy-to-use, domain-specific data processing operations (e.g., filter or combine) that can be mapped onto a multitude of implementations that depend on the context the DPD is used in. Mashup Plans are modeled as shown in Fig. 1. In this paper, we introduce a new approach to transform Mashup Plans into alternative, executable formats depending on the requirements set by the use case scenario. Note that due to the implementation focus of this paper, we are not looking into conceptual details.

The remainder of this paper is structured as follows: in Sect. 2, we describe basic concepts that are necessary to explain our approach. Section 3 describes related work. In Sect. 4, the main contribution of our paper is presented: we introduce an approach for pattern-based Mashup Plan transformation and execution. Section 5 describes the maturity of our tool and Sect. 6 its features. After that, in Sect. 7, the prototypical implementation of our approach is presented, in Sect. 8, the presented demo flow is shown, in Sect. 9 we describe the challenge preparation and the results are subsequently evaluated in Sect. 10. Finally, Sect. 11 summarizes the results and gives an outlook to future work.

2   Basic Concepts

In this section, we describe basic concepts that are necessary to comprehend the approach presented in this paper. These concepts are (i) Mashup Plans, as introduced in previous work, and (ii) the Topology and Orchestration Specification for Cloud Applications (TOSCA) that is used for provisioning of the mashup's execution components in a cloud computing environment.

2.1   Mashup Plans

A Mashup Plan is a non-executable, domain-specific model to define data mashup (i.e., ad-hoc data processing and integration) scenarios and was

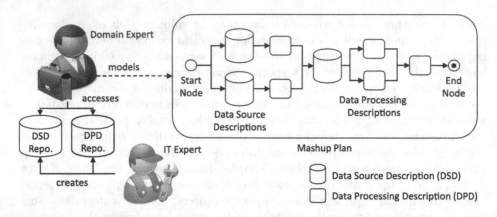

Fig. 1. Overview of Mashup Plans (based on [11])

introduced in our previous work [11]. The modeler of Mashup Plans is usually a domain-expert such as a business person, without any knowledge of technical details. As depicted in Fig. 1, a Mashup Plan is a cohesive, directed flow graph based on the *Pipes and Filter* pattern [15] containing two types of nodes and a single edge type representing the data and control flow between these nodes. The node types are subdivided into Data Source Descriptions (DSD) and Data Processing Descriptions (DPDs) as well as a single start and end node. Data Source Descriptions offer a non-technical way to model data sources, without having to know about low-level details such as data base ports, URLs, etc. These DSDs are based on so called business objects as described by [6,14]. The second type of nodes, the DPDs, describe how the data is processed, i.e., how it is filtered, aggregated, analyzed, or otherwise modified. That is, a DPD describes an operation, i.e., a piece of code, that processes the data. The actual implementation of the DPD depends on its context. As a consequence, different implementations exist for a single DPD, depending on the data types, data structures, etc. The mapping from DSDs and DPDs to their corresponding implementation can be realized by a rule-based approach as described by Reimann et al. [19]. When modeling Mashup Plans, the following restrictions have to be considered: (i) a Mashup Plan contains a single start node to indicate the entry point of the flow, (ii) a completely modeled Mashup Plan contains at least one Data Source Description and at least one Data Processing Description, and (iii) a Mashup Plan contains a single output represented by an end node (depicted in Fig. 1). The technical properties of DSDs and DPDs that are used to model Mashup Plans are defined once by IT experts who store them in corresponding repositories. This enables Mashup Plan modeling by domain-experts based on the DSD and DPD repositories without them having to specify any technical details. A concrete example of a modeled Mashup Plan using the FlexMash data mashup tool is depicted in Fig. 5(a).

Note that we slightly modified the concept of Mashup Plans in this paper in contrast to previous work by adding the start node. In previous work, the entry point of Mashup Plans was defined through the data source descriptions. As a consequence, DSDs could not contain incoming connections and represented the starting points of the flow. However, in some use cases it is necessary to integrate data sources not only in the beginning but also within the flow (e.g., the Twitter data source in Fig. 5(a)). As a consequence, we added the start node to the Mashup Plan.

2.2 TOSCA

In this section, basic concepts of the Topology and Orchestration Specification for Cloud Applications (TOSCA) are introduced that are necessary to comprehend the approach presented in this paper. The following section is based on [10].

TOSCA is a standard of OASIS to describe cloud applications in a portable way. TOSCA-based descriptions define (i) the structure as well as (ii) the management functionalities of cloud-based applications. Although TOSCA is a relatively new standard, several tools exist that ease modeling, provisioning, and management of TOSCA-based applications. The open source ecosystem *Open-TOSCA*, for example, includes a graphical modeling tool called *Winery* [13] and a plan-based provisioning and management runtime environment [3], which can be used to provision and manage TOSCA applications fully automatically. Further details on the TOSCA standard can be found in the official OASIS TOSCA specification [16], TOSCA Primer [17], or Binz et al. [2].

The core of the application description in TOSCA is the *Topology Template*, a directed graph containing *Node Templates* (vertices) and *Relationship Templates* (edges). Node Templates may describe all components of an application, including all software and hardware components. The relations between those Node Templates are represented by Relationship Templates. Node and Relationship Templates are typed by *Node Types* and *Relationship Types*, respectively. Types define the semantics of the templates, as well as their properties, provided management operations, and so on. Types can be refined or extended by an inheritance mechanism. *TOSCA Policies* are used to define non-functional requirements for the provisioning of an application. Using TOSCA Policies, it is possible to determine costs, security, availability, scalability or similar non-functional requirements. TOSCA specifies an exchange format called *Cloud Service Archive* (CSAR) to package Topology Templates, types, associated artifacts, plans, and all required files into one self-contained package. This package is portable across different standards-compliant TOSCA runtime environments [4].

3 Related Work

In the past, many data mashup solutions have been introduced in science and industry that are built to enable an ad-hoc processing and integration of data. Usually these solutions offer a graphical modeling tool that enables the users to define data sources and data operations as well as the way data is processed.

Well-known examples are *Yahoo! Pipes*[1], *Intel MashMaker*[2] and the *IBM Infosphere MashupHub*[3]. These enterprise-ready solutions offer a lot of functionality in regard to the data sources they are able to integrate as well as the data processing operations they support. However, existing solutions only offer a single possibility for execution, i.e., they have a single, static implementation. Nowadays, the user requirements may differ significantly, especially when it comes to data processing and integration. In production environments, for example, it is very important that data is processed in *real-time*, i.e., a very efficient execution has to be supported. Furthermore, in businesses, for example, robustness and security are very important aspects. In other scenarios, the coping with huge amounts of data has to be supported, and so on. However, current mashup solutions cannot cope with these heterogeneous requirements. In this paper, we tackle this issue by introducing a flexible data mashup execution based on user requirements.

Furthermore, existing approaches define abstract, non-technical models to describe data processing and integration scenarios similar to the introduced Mashup Plans. However, oftentimes these approaches do not offer a sufficient abstraction from technical details. For example, many modeling nodes in *Yahoo! Pipes* require the knowledge of programming concepts such as string builders, regular expressions, HTML scraping, *for each*-loops, and so on. This limits the usage to software developers that have to know about technical details. Using so called *business objects* [6,14], we can enable modeling data mashup scenarios based on the user's domain. This further enables a widely usable data mashup solution, e.g., for business users and for technical experts as well.

In previous work [11], we already introduced the modeling of Mashup Plans as well as some basic ideas of their transformation. These Mashup Plans can be modeled using a variety of different formats, e.g., also using established standards such as BPMN, XML or JSON. All these abstract languages have to be further transformed onto an executable level as described in Sect. 4.2. As a consequence, Mashup Plans offer a generic means to define data mashup scenarios and are not bound to a specific format. In this paper, we focus on the transformation of this model to an executable representation based on patterns, and we describe how these concepts were applied during the ICWE Mashup Challenge 2015.

4   Flexible Data Mashups Based on Pattern-Based Model Transformation

This section describes our proposed mashup approach: flexible data mashups based on pattern-based model transformation. We subdivide the approach into five main steps as depicted in Fig. 2: (i) the modeling of Mashup Plans, (ii) the selection of transformation patterns, (iii) the pattern-based transformation of Mashup Plans into an executable format, (iv) the cloud-based data mashup execution based on user requirements, and (v) the storage and/or visualization

---

[1] https://pipes.yahoo.com/pipes/.
[2] http://intel.ly/1BW2crD.
[3] http://ibm.co/1Ghxv27.

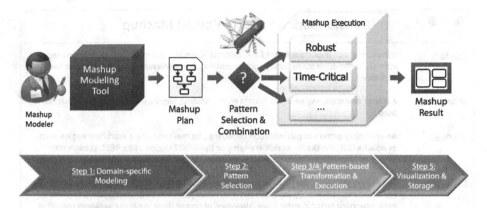

Fig. 2. Overall approach of flexible data mashups (based on [11])

of the derived result. These overall steps are based on previous work [11]. Note that in the following, the terms *pattern* and *transformation pattern* are used synonymously.

After modeling of the Mashup Plan that defines the data as well as how it is processed and integrated, the user can select patterns that represent his/her requirements for the mashup execution. That is, each pattern can fulfill certain user requirements, such as efficiency or robustness. The transformation of the domain-specific, non-executable model to an executable representation is done based on the selected patterns. Finally, the mashup is executed in a suitable engine. The result of the execution can be stored or visualized.

The modeling of Mashup Plans (Step 1) has already been described in previous work, as a consequence, the Mashup Plan modeling step depicted in Fig. 2 will not be described here. Its description can be found in [11]. Furthermore, the use of the mashup result (Step 5) is mostly application-dependent and therefore out of scope of this paper.

4.1 Step 2: Transformation Pattern Selection

In this section, we introduce the transformation patterns, how they are selected and how they can be parameterized. Patterns are high-level descriptions of established practices to solve reoccurring problems. Each pattern can be implemented in a different fashion, i.e., patterns offer an abstract solution to specific problems and can be mapped onto corresponding solution implementations [8]. Each of the *transformation patterns* introduced in this paper fulfills certain user requirements for the data mashup execution.

During modeling of the Mashup Plan, the modeler has the possibility to select the patterns him/herself based on his or her requirements. In case the Mashup Plan modeler is a business person without any knowledge of the specific technical requirements, this decision can also be made by (IT) experts supporting the modeler by analyzing the mashup scenario. To be able to select a pattern,

🏋	Transformation Pattern: Robust Mashup
Problem:	Robustness is an **important factor** for IT systems, especially in **enterprise applications** and systems. It stands for many factors such as **stability, error tolerance, logging** etc. that have to be fulfilled in a robust environment.
Solution:	A **robust execution engine** that supports error handling, logging as well as data persistence is used.
Example:	An exemplary pattern implementation could, e.g., be realized using a **workflow engine** such as Apache ODE, the Oracle workflow engine or the WSO2 engine using BPEL as execution language. These engines **provide all the necessary factors** to ensure robustness.
Evaluation:	The Robust Mashup pattern can be used in enterprise environments in which, e.g., workflows are already established. By using this pattern, **robustness can be guaranteed** which is the most important factor in enterprises. However, of course there are some **setbacks regarding runtime efficiency**.
Combination:	Secure Mashup Pattern; Big Data Mashup Pattern;

Fig. 3. Example of a pattern catalog entry – Robust Mashup

the modeler has to know about all existing patterns, know about their abilities as well as their limitations. Furthermore, the modeler has to know how these patterns can be combined in a reasonable manner. To enable this, we created an extendable pattern catalog that describes widely used patterns regarding data mashup processing. Each entry in this catalog describes a single transformation pattern and has the following content: (i) a description containing the **problem** that is solved by the pattern, (ii) the **solution** the pattern offers to solve this problem, (iii) an **example** how the pattern can be applied, (iv) a short **evaluation**, and (v) information about if and how it can be **combined** with other transformation patterns. When selecting a pattern, the user usually has to define additional parameters that are necessary to find a corresponding implementation. For example, when selecting the time-critical mashup pattern, the user has to specify the maximal time the execution may take. When selecting the robust mashup pattern, the user e.g., has to specify whether error handling is needed, logging has to be supported, etc. This parameterization is done during the pattern's selection. An exemplary entry of the pattern catalog is shown in Fig. 3. As depicted, it contains a textual description of how the pattern can be applied. The selected patterns influence the manner the mashup is executed, e.g., when the depicted pattern *Robust Mashup* is selected from the pattern catalog, the mashup is executed in a robust manner, e.g., using a workflow engine. That is, the selected patterns give a directive for the executable format the mashup plan is transformed into and, as a consequence, for the execution components.

4.2   Step 3: Pattern-Based Transformation

In this section, we describe how the non-executable Mashup Plan is transformed into an executable representation based on patterns. The executable format the

Mashup Plan is transformed into, depends on the patterns that were selected in the previous step. The mapping of the Mashup Plan onto the executable model as well as the selection of the execution engine that is being used to execute it, is chosen using a rule-based transformation approach, similar to the one described by [18,19]. To structure patterns and connect them to corresponding implementations, we use so called *pattern graphs*. A pattern graph is a tree-based, directed graph containing nodes and edges. A node in the pattern graph represents either a pattern or an implementation. An edge from one node to another represents a specialization. There are two types of edges. The *"consists of"* edge is used to connect patterns and indicates that a pattern consists of several sub-patterns. As a consequence, the problem described by the pattern can only be solved, if all of its sub-patterns are applied. The second edge type *"implemented by"* is used to connect to the implementation nodes. If a pattern is connected to one or more implementations, it means that it can be realized by either one of them. In this case, one of them has to be selected either manually or automatically.

To summarize, a generic pattern at the root node of the tree is getting more and more concrete by being subdivided into sub-patterns and finally into implementation fragments. As a consequence, patterns can be structured hierarchically through different abstraction levels. Furthermore, a single pattern can be realized by different implementations. The root node of the pattern graph represents the most abstract pattern, which is the pattern described textually in the pattern catalog. That is, a different pattern graph exists for each entry of the pattern catalog. Which path in the pattern graph is chosen in order to reach the implementation at the leaf nodes, depends on the pattern's parameterization. This decision is made based on rules that are evaluated during traversal of the

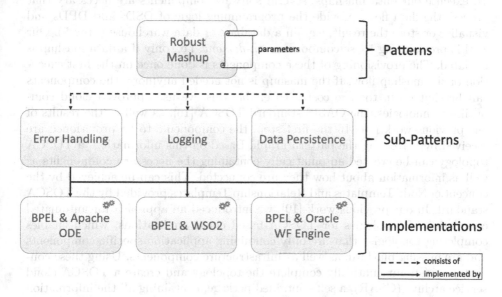

Fig. 4. Pattern graph example

pattern graph. These rules compare the parameters of the pattern with predefined properties of the implementations to find the most suitable one. Note that our approach will always find an implementation, however, it is not guaranteed that it can fulfill all given user requirements. In this case, the user has to decide whether to use the selected implementation or not. An exemplary pattern graph for the *Robust Mashup* pattern is depicted in Fig. 4.

Note that for a single selected pattern, this rule-based transformation approach can be applied in a straight-forward manner. However, if several patterns are combined, the determination of a suitable pattern implementation is much more complex and is currently part of our ongoing work.

Once a suitable implementation is found, the transformation of the Mashup Plan to a suitable executable representation can be processed. We use predefined, modularized implementation fragments that are scripted together to create the executable model. For example, if the execution is done using a workflow engine, we can create the executable workflow automatically using, e.g., invoke nodes of the Business Process Execution Language (BPEL) to execute the operations defined in the Mashup Plan. The programming logic of the DSDs and DPDs is stored in code fragments, e.g. Java Web Services that are executed by the workflow. In other examples, e.g., when using the Node-RED[4] execution engine, the transformation works in a similar fashion by connecting predefined, JavaScript code fragments. The implemented pattern transformations for the ICWE Rapid Mashup Challenge are described in Sect. 9.

4.3   Step 4: TOSCA-Based Deployment and Execution

To execute our data mashups, several software components are necessary that process the data flow, provide the programming logic of DSDs and DPDs and visualize or store the result, e.g., in a database or data warehouse (Step 5). Our goal is provisioning these components *on-demand*, i.e., only if a data mashup is initiated. The provisioning of these components is done once on the first execution of the mashup flow. If the mashup is not needed anymore, the components can be shut down to save costs. To enable this, we use approved cloud computing technologies, the OASIS standard TOSCA [16], as well as the results of our previous work [10]. In the first step, the components to be provisioned are received by traversing the pattern graph. Based on this information, a TOSCA topology can be created automatically containing the necessary components as well as information about how they are connected. This can be achieved by the concept of Node Templates and Relationship Templates provided by the TOSCA standard. In our previous work [10], we introduced an approach for automated completion of topologies for TOSCA-based cloud applications, which enables completing topologies that are only containing application-specific components and are missing platform as well as infrastructure components. Using these concepts, we can automatically complete the topology and create a TOSCA cloud service archive (CSAR), a self-contained package, containing all the information

---

[4] http://nodered.org/.

and software components necessary to provision applications in a cloud environment. For example, if the implementation contains a workflow engine to be provisioned, the necessary components to run it, such as a web server, an operating system and an instance of a cloud provider are added automatically to the topology and, as a consequence, to the CSAR. Using the plan generator extension of our TOSCA runtime OpenTOSCA [4], this cloud service archive can be used for an automated deployment of the components in the cloud. The automated deployment and execution of the mashup can be initiated using *management plans*, as described by [5]. The interested reader is referred to [2,3,10] and [16] for more information about TOSCA and the OpenTOSCA ecosystem. The implementation of these concepts is part of our ongoing work.

5 FlexMash – Level of Maturity

This section describes the current maturity of the implementation of our previously described approach. We implemented a prototype of FlexMash and used it in two different use case scenarios besides the one for the ICWE Rapid Mashup Challenge described in Sect. 7. In the first scenario, sensor data is integrated and processed to determine high-level situations in smart environments. For this implementation, we developed our prototype to support the stream-based processing of sensor data. The detailed results are described in [9]. The second use case implements a data mashup for exception escalation in advanced manufacturing environments, which is described in [12]. In this use case, exceptions in manufacturing environments are recognized and analyzed based on different data sources. The executed data mashup provides a result to find and solve occurred problems in an efficient manner by processing and integrating the corresponding data of the sources.

The current version of our prototype is tailored to these use cases. However, it offers a high degree of extensibility, which enables an easy adding of different data sources, data operations, patterns, execution formats and engines.

6 FlexMash – Feature Checklist

In this section, the features of the current state of FlexMash's implementation are described based on the ICWE Rapid Mashup Challenge checklist, which contains information about important properties and design choices of mashup tools to enable their categorization. The feature checklist is based on related work and is subdivided into two parts: (i) an overall *mashup feature checklist* as described in [7] (Chap. 6), and (ii) *a mashup tool feature checklist* as described in [1]. The detailed information about the single entries are provided in these references.

– Mashup Feature Checklist
  - **Mashup Type:** Data mashups
  - **Component Type:** Data components
  - **Runtime Location:** Both client and server

- **Integration Logic:** Orchestrated integration
- **Instantiation Lifecycle:** Stateless
- Mashup Tool Feature Checklist
  - **Targeted End-User:** Non programmers
  - **Automation Degree:** Semi-automation
  - **Liveness Level:** Level 3 – Automatic compilation and deployment, requires re-initialization
  - **Interaction Technique:** Visual language (Iconic)
  - **Online User Community:** None (yet)

7   ICWE Rapid Mashup Challenge – Mashup Scenario

In this section, we introduce the scenario that was implemented and presented during the ICWE Rapid Mashup Challenge 2015. For this challenge, we introduced a specific mashup scenario according to the requirements. The goal of the challenge was integrating specific data sources in an *"elegant"* manner using new mashup tools and approaches. The choices of the data sources were as follows: (i) the New York Times API[5], which can be used to receive articles and other news items, (ii) the YouTube API[6] to integrate video data, as well as (iii) the Google Maps API[7] to display geo locations in the Google Maps user interface. At least one of these APIs had to be chosen and at least two data sources had to be processed and integrated in total. As a consequence, it was allowed to add other web APIs arbitrarily. Due to our tool – respectively our prototypical implementation – being a pure data mashup tool that cannot yet handle video data and does not focus on the user interface, we used the New York Times web API and the Twitter API[8] as second data source for the challenge.

Based on these data sources, our scenario finds out the sentiment of people on articles of the New York Times website. To retrieve these sentiment information, we use corresponding Tweets that address the article's topic. To achieve this, simple integration techniques are not sufficient. It is necessary to use sophisticated data analytics techniques, which can be achieved by using the concept of the previously introduced DPDs. Firstly, a named entity recognition DPD is required to search the articles for keywords that can be used to find corresponding Tweets. Furthermore, a sentiment analysis has to be conducted based on the found Tweets to receive the overall sentiment of an article. To model such a complicated data mashup scenario, the user can make use of the introduced Mashup Plans and create a graphical description using DSDs and DPDs. This description can then be used to create different executable representations as described in Sect. 4. The graphical model for this scenario is displayed in Fig. 5(a). This scenario has also been used for the runtime measurements described in Sect. 10. The execution semantics of the demo flow is described in the following Sect. 8.

---

[5] http://www.nytimes.com/services/xml/rss/index.html.
[6] http://www.youtube.com/yt/dev/api-resources.html.
[7] https://developers.google.com/maps/.
[8] https://dev.twitter.com/.

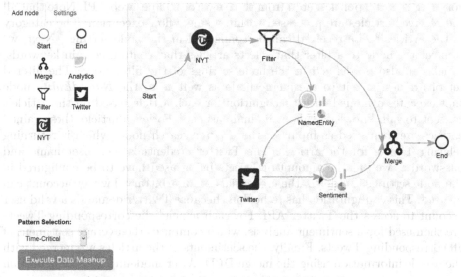

(a) Screenshot of the demo flow used for the challenge

Article	Keywords	Overall Sentiment	Example Tweets
Blue Jays 4, Yankees 0: Russell Martin Crushes Pitch, and Yankees Hopes (link)	Baseball, Toronto Blue Jays, New York Yankees	Sentiment is Neutral!	

(Sentiment Score: 0)

(Sentiment Score: 0)

(b) Visualized result of the challenge mashup

Fig. 5. Screenshots of FlexMash's Mashup Plan modeling and result view

8 Demo Flow

Figure 5(a) depicts the flow we modeled during the ICWE Rapid Mashup Challenge. This flow is representing the scenario that was described in Sect. 7. First, a start node is added to the model. This is necessary to define the entry point of the flow-based model during execution. This start node is connected to a data source description *NYT* that receives all current articles of a corresponding category (e.g., sports, politics, etc.) from the New York Times web API. Note that all the received articles are processed within a single flow execution. The category of the articles to be received can be configured in the node settings. Next, we connect the node to a filter that selects articles that contain certain keywords, which can also be defined in the node settings of the filter node. The filtered set of articles is sent to the merge node as well as to the *NamedEntity* node that executes a named entity recognition for each article based on the article's content to gain knowledge about its main aspects. For each article, these gained entities are then used as input for the *Twitter* search node, which is returning relating Tweets for the articles. The Twitter credentials, i.e., user name and password as well as the amount of Tweets being used have to be configured in the node settings. To do so, the credentials of an arbitrary Twitter account can be used. This configuration has to be done because Twitter demands a valid user account to access the Twitter API. For each article, the corresponding Tweets are then used for a sentiment analysis, which computes the average sentiment of all corresponding Tweets. Finally, the sentiments of the articles are merged with the article information using the merge DPD. After modeling and configuration

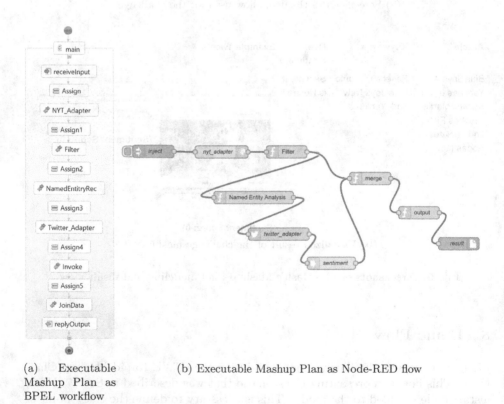

(a)   Executable Mashup Plan as BPEL workflow

(b) Executable Mashup Plan as Node-RED flow

Fig. 6. Different implementations of the challenge's executable Mashup Plan

of the nodes, the user selects *Execute Data Mashup* to run the flow. The output of the flow is the generated HTML web site depicted in Fig. 5(b) containing a list of all processed articles, including their topics, the result of the named entity analysis, the computed average sentiment of an article and some example Tweets that were used for sentiment analysis. As described in Sect. 4, the Mashup Plan is transformed into executable representations based on patterns. In the demo, we implemented the robust pattern using BPEL workflows executed in the ApacheODE[9] workflow engine as well as the time-critical pattern using JSON-based Node-RED flows executed in the Node-RED runtime. The transformed models are depicted in Fig. 6.

9   Challenge Preparations

This section describes the preparations for the challenge and gives an insight into implementation details. An overview of FlexMash's architecture specific to the implementation for the challenge is depicted in Fig. 7. Similar to other mashup tools, FlexMash is hosted online and can be accessed through a web browser. By providing FlexMash as a service on a cloud computing infrastructure (IBM Bluemix[10]), it can be accessed, deployed and scaled easily. The architecture contains four main components. First, the Mashup Plan Modeler (also depicted in Fig. 5(a)) that enables the user to define how the data is stepwise processed. Furthermore, in this component patterns can be viewed and

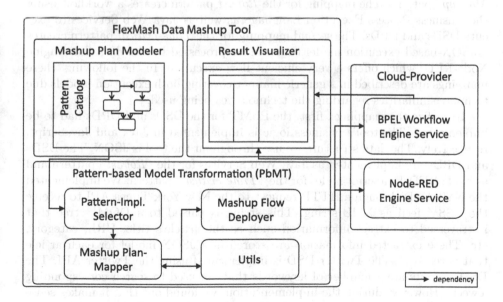

Fig. 7. FlexMash architecture specific to the implemented scenario

---

[9] http://ode.apache.org/.
[10] www.bluemix.net.

selected. Second, the *Pattern-based Model Transformation component (PbMT)* contains the pattern-implementation selector that automatically chooses a suitable implementation for parameterized patterns using a pattern graph-based and rule-based approach as described in Sect. 4.2. For the challenge implementation, the pattern-implementation mapping is kept simple due to the fact that only a single implementation exists for each pattern. The PbMT furthermore contains the logic of the mapping of the Mashup Plan to the executable representation depending on the pattern implementation as well as the logic of the deployment of this model onto a suitable engine. The *Utils* component contains methods supporting this functionality. The execution engines to execute the resulting model are not part of FlexMash, but cloud-based external services. Finally, the fourth component is used for visualization of the engine's output, i.e., the execution result.

To prepare for this challenge, many implementation tasks had to be dealt with. Firstly, the existing user interface of our tool – which is based on the JavaScript framework AlloyUI[11] – had to be adjusted to the newly added data source descriptions and data processing descriptions used for the challenge. This task could be completed in a short time due to the framework's high extensibility.

As described in Sect. 4, the non-executable Mashup Plan is transformed into different execution models depending on patterns that are selected after modeling. For this challenge, we implemented two mappings onto different executable models. Each of these mappings fulfills the requirements of a single pattern. The two patterns we implemented were the *"Robust Mashup"* and the *"Time-critical Mashup"* pattern. The mapping for the *Robust* pattern creates a workflow using the Business Process Execution Language as well as Java Web Services to execute DSDs and DPDs. The second mapping for the *Time-critical* pattern creates a JSON-based execution model that can be processed by the data flow engine Node-RED, which offers a very efficient flow execution. In the following, these mappings are described in a generic manner covering both execution models due to many similarities regarding the technologies being used.

To realize the mappings, first, the PbMT for the DSDs and DPDs had to be implemented. The tool's business logic is implemented in Java and JavaScript, respectively. The data structure we use throughout the tool is JSON. The DSDs and DPDs are implemented as Java Web Services for the *"Robust"* pattern and as Node-RED JavaScript nodes for the *"Time-critical"* pattern. We implemented the NYT DSD through a HTTP request to the New York Times API to receive the RSS[12] feed as XML string. This string is parsed to a DOM[13] tree that is traversed to extract information such as the article's title, URL, category, etc. These extracted information are stored in a JSON model for each article that is received. The Twitter DSD is implemented using the Twitter API. The DSD's inputs are a number of keywords that are used to search corresponding Tweets. However, during the implementation, we found out that it makes sense

---

[11] http://alloyui.com/.
[12] Really Simple Syndication.
[13] Document Object Model.

to limit the keywords to a maximum of five. Otherwise, the search for suitable Tweets takes too much time. The received Tweets are also stored in a JSON data structure. After implementing the DSDs, we implemented the DPDs that are able to filter, merge and analyze the data.

The filter DPD used to extract articles containing specific keywords was implemented in a straight-forward manner. The article's text as well as the title is checked for containment of the given keywords using the means of the respective programming language. If it contains one or more of the keywords, it is added to the list of filter results. Next, we implemented the two analytics DPDs, i.e., the named entity recognition and the sentiment analysis. For the named entity recognition, we used libraries provided by the Apache UIMA framework[14]. After a tokenization of the text, the named entities can be extracted automatically. The output of the named entity recognition is also stored in the JSON model. The sentiment analysis is conducted using the library LingPipe[15]. Finally, the merge node was implemented by traversing and integrating the JSON model. For the execution, we currently use execution engine services by the platform-as-a-service provider IBM Bluemix.

The result of the Mashup is visualized in a web user interface, which is based on HTML and JavaScript.

10   Discussion and Findings

During the implementation of our tool for the ICWE Rapid Mashup Challenge, we encountered several issues that are described and discussed in this section. We had some complications with the web APIs we used for this challenge. Firstly, we encountered the issue that the Twitter API is limited to a fixed amount of 180 Tweets every 15 min. As a consequence, we had to severely reduce the number of Tweets to be analyzed per article. However, this led to non-optimal results because usually a large amount of Tweets is necessary to compute the sentiment reliably. Furthermore, we identified weaknesses and limitations of the Twitter search and the sentiment analysis. The Twitter search seems to return advertisement, sometimes not even related to the topic we searched for. The sentiment analysis only uses single words to compute a Tweet's sentiment without involving its context. As a consequence, the results of the Mashup we presented varied in their quality. We got some good results, however, some of the results were obviously wrong or imprecise. Due to the fact that the cause of these issues can be found in external components, the overall mashup approach could convince in regard to functionality, flexibility and powerfulness.

Table 1 displays the runtime measurements we conducted on the demo implementation presented at the ICWE Rapid Mashup Challenge. As depicted, the deployment and transformation time (which also contains the pattern-implementation selection) is nearly the same for the two execution formats being used. This can be explained by the fact that the transformation logic is very

---

[14] https://uima.apache.org/.
[15] http://alias-i.com/lingpipe/.

Table 1. Runtime Measurements

Transf. Pattern	Transformation Time Ø	Deployment Time Ø	Execution Time Ø
Robust	283,4 ms	193,8 ms	2382 ms
Time-Critical	222,8 ms	140,6 ms	23,4 ms

similar in both cases. The deployment of the executable model in the engine is also similar for these pattern implementations, however, it strongly depends on the location and efficiency of the engine being used. The main aspect, the execution time, differs greatly when comparing the two implementations. The robust execution has a high runtime due to the heavy-weight workflow engine that is being used. Additional features such as orchestration, web service calls and exception handling lead to a significant overhead. In contrast, the execution of the time-critical Mashup enables a very low runtime. This can be explained by the light-weight, JavaScript and NodeJS[16]-based implementation, executed in the Node-RED runtime engine, which enables efficient processing of data flows.

We are aware that the benefits of our pattern-based transformation approach do not out-stand in this use case, because there were no requirements such as robustness or efficiency defined in this challenge. However, even though the challenge use case was not completely suitable for our approach, FlexMash could convince us as well as the jurors of the challenge.

11   Summary and Outlook

In this paper, we presented FlexMash, an approach and tool implementation for flexible data mashups based on pattern-based model transformation. By subdividing the data mashup into four abstraction levels, namely, the modeling, transformation, execution and presentation level, we enabled an abstraction from the non-technical, domain-specific modeling of data integration and processing scenarios to the technical execution and finally the visualization and storage of the derived result. By doing so, we enabled a flexible approach through the use of transformation patterns, which leads to a data mashup execution specific to user requirements. As a consequence, we were able to create a generically applicable data mashup solution, suitable for different data sources and data processing operations usable in various use case scenarios. The evaluation of our approach was done by a prototypical implementation that was presented during the ICWE Rapid Mashup Challenge 2015 and by corresponding runtime measurements.

In the future, we are extending our pattern catalog as well as the corresponding pattern implementations. Furthermore, we will introduce *modeling patterns* to make the modeling of Mashup Plans even more domain-specific and easy-to-use.

Acknowledgment. This work is supported by the Deutsche Forschungsgemeinschaft (DFG, German Research Foundation) within the project SitOPT (Grant 610872).

---

[16] https://nodejs.org/.

References

1. Aghaee, S., Nowak, M., Pautasso, C.: Reusable decision space for mashup tool design. In: 4th ACM SIGCHI Symposium on Engineering Interactive Computing Systems (EICS 2012), Copenhagen, Denmark, pp. 211–220, June 2012
2. Binz, T., Breitenbücher, U., Kopp, O., Leymann, F.: TOSCA: portable automated deployment and management of cloud applications. In: Advanced Web Services, pp. 527–549. Springer, New York, January 2014
3. Binz, T., Breitenbücher, U., Haupt, F., Kopp, O., Leymann, F., Nowak, A., Wagner, S.: OpenTOSCA – a runtime for TOSCA-based cloud applications. In: Basu, S., Pautasso, C., Zhang, L., Fu, X. (eds.) ICSOC 2013. LNCS, vol. 8274, pp. 692–695. Springer, Heidelberg (2013)
4. Breitenbücher, et al.: Combining declarative and imperative cloud application provisioning based on TOSCA. In: IC2E, pp. 87–96. IEEE, March 2014
5. Breitenbücher, U., Binz, T., Leymann, F.: A method to automate cloud application management patterns. In: Proceedings of the Eighth International Conference on Advanced Engineering Computing and Applications in Sciences (ADVCOMP 2014), pp. 140–145. Xpert Publishing Services, August 2014
6. Cohn, D., et al.: Business artifacts: a data-centric approach to modeling business operations and processes. Bull. IEEE Comput. Soc. Techn. Committee Data Eng. **32**(3), 3–9 (2009)
7. Daniel, F., Matera, M.: Mashups - Concepts, Models and Architectures. Data-Centric Systems and Applications. Springer, Heidelberg (2014)
8. Falkenthal, M., et al.: From pattern languages to solution implementations. In: Proceedings of the Sixth International Conferences on Pervasive Patterns and Applications (PATTERNS 2014), Venice, Italy (2014)
9. Hirmer, P., Wieland, M., Schwarz, H., Mitschang, B., Breitenbücher, U., Leymann, F.: SitRS - a situation recognition service based on modeling and executing situation templates. In: Proceedings of the 9th Symposium and Summer School on Service-Oriented Computing (SUMMERSOC 2015) (2015)
10. Hirmer, P., Breitenbücher, U., Binz, T., Leymann, F.: Automatic topology completion of TOSCA-based cloud applications. In: Proceedings des CloudCycle14 Workshops auf der 44. Jahrestagung der Gesellschaft für Informatik e.V. (GI). LNI, vol. 232, pp. 247–258. Gesellschaft für Informatik e.V. (GI) (2014)
11. Hirmer, P., Reimann, P., Wieland, M., Mitschang, B.: Extended techniques for flexible modeling and execution of data mashups. In: Proceedings of the 4th International Conference on Data Management Technologies and Applications (DATA), April 2015
12. Kassner, L.B., Mitschang, B.: MaXCept-decision support in exception handling through unstructured data integration in the production context. An integral part of the smart factory. In: Proceedings of the 48th Hawaii International Conference on System Sciences (2015)
13. Kopp, O., Binz, T., Breitenbücher, U., Leymann, F.: Winery – a modeling tool for TOSCA-based cloud applications. In: Basu, S., Pautasso, C., Zhang, L., Fu, X. (eds.) ICSOC 2013. LNCS, vol. 8274, pp. 700–704. Springer, Heidelberg (2013)
14. Künzle, V., et al.: PHILharmonicFlows: towards a framework for object-aware process management. J. Softw. Mainten. Evol.: Res. Pract. **23**(4), 205–244 (2011)
15. Meunier, R.: The pipes and filters architecture. In: Pattern Languages of Program Design, pp. 427–440. ACM Press/Addison-Wesley Publishing Co. (1995)
16. OASIS: Topology and Orchestration Specification for Cloud Applications (2013)

17. OASIS: TOSCA Primer, November 2013. http://docs.oasis-open.org/tosca/tosca-primer/v1.0/cnd01/tosca-primer-v1.0-cnd01.pdf
18. Reimann, P., et al.: Data Patterns to Alleviate the Design of Scientific Work Flows Exemplified by a Bone Simulation. In: Proceedings of the 26th International Conference on Scientific and Statistical Database Management (2014)
19. Reimann, P., Schwarz, H., Mitschang, B.: A pattern approach to conquer the data complexity in simulation workflow design. In: Meersman, R., Panetto, H., Dillon, T., Missikoff, M., Liu, L., Pastor, O., Cuzzocrea, A., Sellis, T. (eds.) OTM 2014. LNCS, vol. 8841, pp. 21–38. Springer, Heidelberg (2014)

Interactive, Live Mashup Development Through UI-Oriented Computing

Anis Nouri and Florian Daniel[✉]

University of Trento, Via Sommarive 9, 38123 Povo, TN, Italy
anis.nouri-1@studenti.unitn.it, daniel@disi.unitn.it

Abstract. This paper proposes to approach the problem of developing mashups by exclusively focusing on the Surface Web, that is, the data and functionality accessible through common Web pages. Typically, mashups focus on the integration of resources accessible through the Deep Web, such as data feeds, Web services and Web APIs, that do not have own UIs – next to data extracted from Web pages. Yet, these resources can be wrapped with ad-doc UIs, suitably instrumented, and made accessible through the Surface Web. Doing so enables a UI-oriented computing paradigm that allows developers to implement mashups interactively and in a live fashion inside their Web browser, without having to program any line of code. The goal of this paper is to showcase UI-oriented computing in practice and to demonstrate its feasibility and potential.

Keywords: UI-oriented computing · iAPIs · Mashups · Integration

1 Introduction

The most notable technologies today to publish and access data and functionality over the Web are SOAP/WSDL Web services [2], RESTful Web services [12], RSS/Atom feeds, and static XML/JSON/CSV resources. Alternatively, data may be rendered in and scraped from HTML Web pages, for example, using tools like Dapper (http://open.dapper.net) or similar that publish extracted content again via any of the previous technologies. W3C widgets [4] or Java portlets [1] are technologies for the reuse of small, full-fledged applications that also provide for the reuse of user interfaces (UIs).

All these technologies (except the Web pages) are oriented toward programmers, and understanding the underlying abstractions and usage conventions requires significant software development expertise. This makes data integration a prerogative of skilled programmers, turns it into a complex and time-consuming endeavor (even for small integration scenarios), and prevents less skilled users from getting the best value out of the opportunities available on the Web.

UI-oriented computing (UIC [8]) takes a different perspective and starts from the UIs of applications we all – programmers and users – are accustomed with and that are free of developer-oriented abstractions. The research question UIC poses is if and, if yes, which of the conventional Web engineering tasks can be

© Springer International Publishing Switzerland 2016
F. Daniel and C. Pautasso (Eds.): RMC 2015, CCIS 591, pp. 31–49, 2016.
DOI: 10.1007/978-3-319-28727-0_3

achieved if we start from the UIs of applications, instead of from their APIs or services. The vision is to enable everybody to perform simple integration tasks directly inside their Web browser, for example, the integration of data extracted from different Web pages or the automation of repeated navigation actions.

In our prior work [9], we already investigated how to turn UIs into programmable artifacts and introduced the idea of *interactive APIs* (iAPIs), that is, APIs users can interact with via their graphical Web UIs. In [8], we then studied the specific case of *data integration* and described an end-to-end solution for UI-oriented computing consisting of an iAPI annotation format, a graphical editor for iAPI manipulation and integration, and a suitable runtime environment.

The *goal* of this paper is to showcase a more extensive case study (the one developed in the context of the Rapid Mashup Challenge) and to provide insights into the practical aspects of UI-oriented computing with the current prototype of our development and runtime environments. In particular, the goal is to highlight the benefits to both common users (interactive, live development without coding) and programmers (programmatic UIC via a dedicated JavaScript library).

Next (Sects. 2 and 3), we introduce the concept and practice of UI-oriented computing along with its underlying runtime infrastructure. In Sect. 4, we then introduce the scenario we selected to approach the Rapid Mashup Challenge and how we prepared for the Challenge. In Sect. 5, we then describe the step-by-step development of the mashup scenario using the UI-oriented computing approach. We conclude the paper with a discussion of a set of works that are related to the proposal we push forward in this paper and a discussion of the findings, lessons learned and future works.

2   UI-Oriented Computing

The idea of UIC is to propose a new kind of "abstraction": no abstraction. The intuition is to turn UI elements into interactive artifacts that, besides their primary purpose in the page (e.g., rendering data), also serve to access a set of operations that can be performed on the artifacts (e.g., reusing data). Operations can be enacted either interactively, for example, by pointing and clicking elements, choosing options, dragging and dropping them, and similar – all interaction modalities that are native to UIs – or programmatically.

The core ingredient, interactive APIs, come as a binomial of a *microformat* for the annotation of HTML elements with data structures and operations and a *UIC engine* able to interpret the annotations and to run UI-oriented data integrations. The engine is implemented as a browser extension. A dedicated *iAPI editor* injects into the page *graphical controls* that allow the user to specify data integration logics interactively. The UIC engine maps them to a set of iAPI-specific *JavaScript functions* implementing the respective runtime support. The library of JavaScript functions can also be programmed directly by programmers, without the need for interacting with UI elements. To users, the UI elements act as proxies toward the features of the library. A UI-oriented computing *middleware* complements the library; both are part of the browser plug-in. It takes care

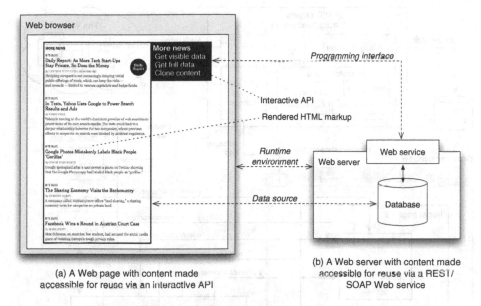

(a) A Web page with content made accessible for reuse via an interactive API

(b) A Web server with content made accessible for reuse via a REST/ SOAP Web service

Fig. 1. Analogy between visual, interactive APIs (iAPIs) and conventional RESTful or SOAP Web services: iAPIs are executed inside the client browser and "programmed" visually and interactively via graphical controls injected into the markup of the page.

of setting up communications among integrated applications (e.g., to load data dynamically from third-party pages) and of storing interactively defined integration logics in the browser's *local storage*. Programmers with access to the source code of a page can inject their JavaScript code directly into it. If a potential source page is not yet annotated to support iAPIs, it is possible to *inject* suitable annotations from the outside and to store them either locally on a remote Web server for reuse and sharing.

For a better understanding, Fig. 1 shows a possible rendering of an iAPI inside a Web page and also draws the parallelisms with conventional APIs, such as RESTful or SOAP Web services. In [8], we discuss how the graphical controls and standard user interactions like drag and drop, point and click, buttons, and similar can be interpreted as programming intentions; the paper specifically focuses on the case of data integration, the scenario we will approach in the Challenge. The paper also provides a detailed description of the iAPI annotation format used in the implementation described in this work.

3   UI-Oriented Computing Infrastructure

Figure 2 shows the internal architecture of the current prototype, which comes as a Google Chrome browser extension. It comes with two core elements: a UIC engine for the execution of UI-oriented data integration logics and an iAPI editor for visual, interactive development. The UIC engine is split into

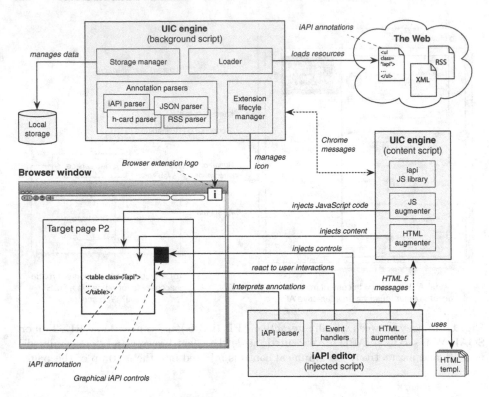

Fig. 2. Architecture of the UI-oriented computing environment as browser extension.

two parts: The *background script* provides core middleware services, such as extension management (via its icon and pop-up menu), remote resource access, data parsing, and local storage management. The *content script* implements the iapi JavaScript library for programmatic UIC (the implementation is based on http://toddmotto.com/mastering-the-module-pattern), injects JavaScript code into the page under development, and provides for the rendering of data (using the jQuery plug-in). Content and background script communicate via Chrome system messages. The iAPI editor comes as JavaScript code that is injected into the Web page under development. It parses the annotations of the iAPIs inside the page, augments them accordingly with graphical controls, and injects the event handlers necessary to intercept user interactions that can be turned into JavaScript data integration logics (in turn, injected into the page by the content script).

As for the features identified in the Call for Participation of the Rapid Mashup Challenge (http://mashup.inf.usi.ch/challenge/2015/checklist. html), UI-oriented computing and the current implementation of the prototypical computing infrastructure support the features summarized in Fig. 3. The essence of UIC is that it aims at the development of applications without the need to code any interaction with APIs or services of the Deep Web, therefore it specifically focuses on UI mashups. Hybrid mashups, i.e., mashups that integrate also application logic and/or data sources, are supported in that application logic can be accessed by automating and making reusable the interaction with HTML forms, and data can be extracted from Web pages (we will use both these features in the Challenge). The core component types the approach focuses on are UI components, the iAPIs, and they are integrated on the client-side inside the Web browser. Some features of the runtime environment, e.g., the persistent storage of external Web page annotations and the form automation service, are hosted on a Web server but integrated inside the client browser. The respective integration logic is UI-based, in line with the vision of UIC, and applications are short-lining. That is, they are applications running inside the client browser, and their runtime lifecycle only depends on the lifetime of the respective browser window: once closed, the application is stopped.

Regarding the features provided by the iAPI editor (the "mashup tool"), it targets end users and aims to enable them to perform simple data integration operations interactively inside their own browser. The JavaScript library for coding iAPI reuse targets programmers. The degree of automation is high for end users (programming instruction are derived automatically from their user interactions and configurations), while coding the JavaScript library is a manual effort. The liveliness level of the resulting development experience is that of dynamic modification, that is, live development inside the browser. The inter-

Checklist	
Mashup Features	**Mashup Tool Features**
Mashup Type:	Targeted End-User:
User Interface (UI) mashups	Non Programmers
Hybrid mashups	Expert Programmers
Component Types:	Automation Degree:
UI components	Semi-automation
Runtime Location:	Manual
Client side only	Liveness Level:
Integration Logic:	Level 4 (Dynamic Modification)
UI-based integration	Interaction Technique:
Instantiation Lifecycle:	WYSIWYG
Short-living	Programming by Demonstration
	Textual DSL
	Online User Community:
	None

Fig. 3. Summary of the features by the proposed UI-oriented computing paradigm.

action technique proposed is WYSIWYG for the users of the iAPI editor (the results of all integration actions are rendered immediately); the recording of user interactions with forms for their automation follows a programming by demonstration approach, which is however again visual and interactive, just like the iAPI editor. Programmers, instead, can rely on a textual DSL implemented as a set of functions provided by the JavaScript library.

4   The Challenge: Scenario and Preparation

Given the set of APIs that can be used in the context of the Rapid Mashup Challenge (Google Maps, Youtube and the New York Times) and the described goals and implementation of the UI-oriented computing approach, we chose to participate in the Challenge with a data integration scenario. Next, we describe the target mashup in more details and explain how we prepared for the Challenge.

Fig. 4. The target data mashup running in the browser.

4.1   Mashup Scenario

We explain the target mashup by means of its screen shot in Fig. 4. The application is a data integration that takes latest technology news from the New York Times (http://www.nytimes.com/) and the Discover Magazine (http://discovermagazine.com/) – news are represented by their title, author and summary – and also provides a translation of the summary from English to Italian using the Yandex Translation API (https://tech.yandex.com/translate/). The two data sources are integrated via a common merge/union operation, while the translation requires iterating over each news article and invoking the translation Web service for each summary. The result is rendered inside the target page of the developer by means of a common HTML table.

4.2 Preparation of Challenge

Mashing up the two data sources and the translation API in the scenario with the proposed UIC paradigm requires some preparation. In general:

1. *Implementing suitable UIs for all resources.* For data and functionality to be extracted from Web pages, the UI is already there. For data feeds, services or APIs, this requires new simple Web front-ends that provide access to the resources' features, e.g., tables visualizing data from feeds or forms allowing users to operate a remote service or API.
2. *Annotating all UIs for reuse.* For existing Web pages this requires injecting annotations into the markup of the pages, e.g., using the interactive iAPI annotator (developed in parallel to the core UI-oriented computing infrastructure) that allows one to inject iAPI annotations into a page at the client-side at page loading time. Newly developed front-ends can directly be annotated in their source markup.

Specifically, this means that we need to annotate the Discover Magazine to enable the extraction of news and to implement an ad-hoc HTML form providing access to the translation API. In addition, we also need to implement an empty target page that will host the integrated data and translations. We do not annotate the New York Times in advance, since we also would like to demonstrate the use of the interactive iAPI annotator during the Challenge. We describe the preparation of the other parts next, starting from the target page.

The screen shot in Fig. 5 illustrates the implementations of the *target page*. The top part is the rendering of the page inside the browser; the lower part reports the source HTML markup of the page. As can be seen in the code, the page does not have any own data to be rendered, and the gray shaded `div` element is marked as an interactive API by the annotation `class="h-iapi"`. This simple annotation is enough to turn the `div` into a UI element users can interact with. In our case, this is the UI element that will host the integrated data. Nothing more is needed to implement the target page.

Figure 6, instead, illustrates the annotated start page of the *Discover Magazine*. The annotation is achieved by means of the iAPI annotator tool, which allows one to annotate interactively a page and to inject annotations on the fly each time the annotated page is accessed. This means that the annotation of the magazine does not require us to download the page and to store it locally; instead only the annotations are stored in a dedicated Web-accessible repository and reused at each access to the page. The specific annotations used to extract news from this page are (used in the `class` attribute of HTML elements):

- `h-iapi`: identifies the area from which to extract content;
- `e-data:News`: categorizes the identified iAPI as a data source and labels it as "News;"
- `e-item:Article`: identifies the DOM nodes that host individual news items and assigns the label "Article" to them;

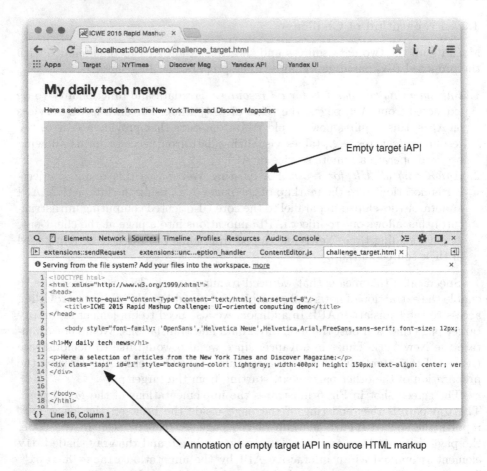

Fig. 5. The empty target mashup running in the browser.

- p-attr:Title, p-attr:Author, p-attr:Summary: identify the different components that make up a news item (the attributes of the item) and labels them as "Title", "Author" and "Summary."

The same annotation structure will be used during the Challenge to annotated the New York Times news items. This allows us to automatically match items at data integration time without the need for transforming input data structures and to save time during the live demonstration.

Finally, Fig. 7 shows the HTML form developed on top of the *Yandex Translation API* (a RESTful Web service). Since we do not directly want to interact with the API itself, the form is needed to make its functionality available through the Surface Web. The form comes with three input fields (text to translate and the input/output languages) that allow the user to translate text by invoking the translation API in the background on behalf of the user. The result is shown on another page after hitting the Translate button. In the next Section, we will

Fig. 6. The annotated Discover Magazine with injected graphical controls.

see how this form can be programmed by example and turned into a piece of reusable business logic for the development of the target mashup.

5   The Challenge: Live Mashup Development

Given the empty target page, the annotated Discover Magazine and the HTML form that provides interactive access to the translation API, we are ready for the development of the mashup to be showcased in the Challenge. The available time to showcase the UI-oriented computing approach and to develop the mashup outlined above is 10 min. We structure the demo into the following steps:

1. Annotation of the New York Times technology news
2. Fetching of news from the New York Times
3. Fetching of and merging with news from the Discover Magazine
4. Rendering of integrated data suing a table representation
5. Programmatic addition of a new column to host the translations
6. Recording of user interactions with the translation form for reuse

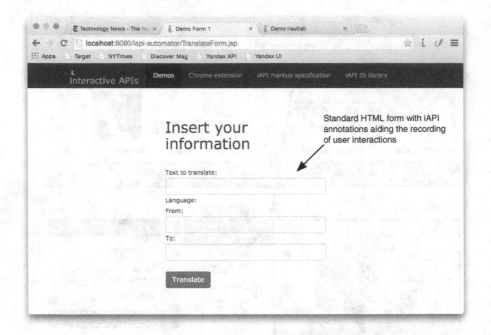

Fig. 7. The auxiliary HTML form developed on top of the Yandex translation API to enable UI-oriented reuse.

7. Programmatic iteration over news and reuse of recorded interactions
8. Rendering of integrated dataset

Next, we describe the demo showcased during the Mashup Challenge step by step and provide the necessary explanations with the help of screen shots.

Figure 8 illustrates the annotation process for the New York Times technology news (❶). We specifically focus on the "More news" area, which is well structured and allows us to easily annotate and extract news items. Clicking on the "i" icon with the pencil in the top right corner of the browser opens the overlay window shown in the lower right part of the screen shot. This window serves as control console for the annotation process. The process is as follows: First, the user identifies the HTML area of interest (this is highlighted in the left-hand side of the screen shot by the rectangular box surrounding the news to be extracted). Then, the user identifies the DOM element that hosts an individual news article (represented by the green-shaded area in the top part of the highlighted area inside the page). The annotator tool automatically identifies all DOM elements with similar structure. Next, the user identifies the individual attributes of each news item by selecting them inside one of the identified news items. Once all attributes are identified, the control panel allows the user to label the data source ("News"), the items ("Article") and the attributes ("Title", "Author", "Summary"). Finalizing the annotation process saves the annotations using a

Selected HTML element of the DOM tree

Control panel for the annotation of identified HTML elements

Fig. 8. Interactive annotation of the New York Times Technology News site (Color figure online).

dedicated Web service and injects them into the page. The newly created iAPI is ready for data extraction.

The reuse of the identified news articles (❷) is now supported via a simple drag and drop action. Figure 9 illustrates the process. When the user moves the mouse over the area marked as iAPI inside the New York Times page, the black graphical controls pop up and allow him/her to pick the data by dragging and dropping the "Get data" menu entry of from the injected menu. Since the target iAPI is still empty, this process fills the iAPI with the extracted data.

The next step of the data integration process (❸) requires the user to repeat a similar drag and drop action using the Discover Magazine, as illustrated in Fig. 10. The key difference from the first action is that now at drag release time

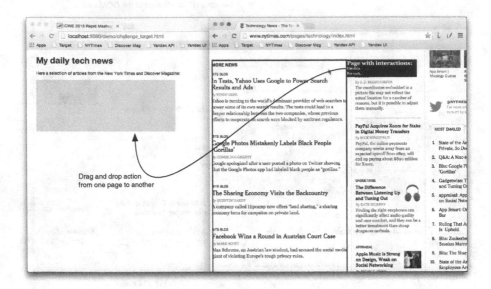

Fig. 9. Dragging and dropping news articles from the New York Times into the target page fills the target iAPI with extracted data and applies a standard visualization format, e.g., a list or table layout.

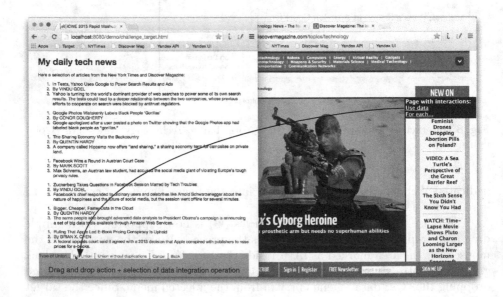

Fig. 10. Dragging and dropping news articles from the Discover Magazine into the target page causes the target iAPI to ask the user which action he/she wants to perform, given that there are already data in the iAPI.

the target iAPI allows the user to specify how to disambiguate his/her action (in fact, multiple interpretations of a drop action on an iAPI that already contains data are possible, e.g., join, merge, substitute, etc.). In our scenario, the user chooses to "merge" the new data with the one already fetched from the New York Times, specifically using a "full union" operator (there is no need to eliminate possible duplicates, as the two data sources are too different and it is unlikely that there will be two articles with exactly the same title, author and summary). A final selection of the table layout from the injected menu of the target iAPI reformats the data fetched from the two data sources as illustrated in the top part of Fig. 11 (❹).

Fig. 11. Programmatic extension of the table with a new column for the translation

To showcase how programmers can leverage on the proposed UI-oriented computing paradigm, we now switch off the interactive iAPI editor that injects graphical controls using the pop up menu that opens when clicking on the extensions logo in the top right of the browser window and turn on the JavaScript console of the browser. This allows the skilled programmer to input UI-oriented programming instructions in JavaScript and to modify the mashup rendered in the browser window on the fly.

The screen shot in Fig. 11 illustrates the first step of the manual development process, i.e., the expansion of the table in the browser with a new column able to host the translations of the summaries (❺). The JavaScript console reports the respective programming instruction. The selector $("#1") is the jQuery (https://jquery.com/) selector that uniquely identifies the target iAPI inside the target page (see Fig. 5). The function addAttribute injects the new column into the iAPI, both into its in-memory data object and its graphical rendering inside the page.

The next step is the translation of the summaries. Doing so requires first recording an exemplary interaction with the translation HTML form we prepared before the Challenge (❻). This process is illustrated in Fig. 12. The recording

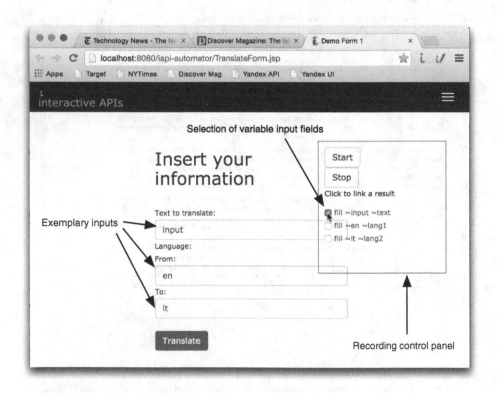

Fig. 12. Recording user interactions with the HTML form providing access to the Yandex translation service. The controls at the right allow the user to start/stop the recording and to identify variable inputs to be filled at invocation time.

control panel allows the user to start and stop the recording and to mark input fields as either constants (the values provided as examples during the recording will also be used when replaying the recorded interactions) or variables (the values of these can be provided as dynamic inputs each time recorded interactions are replayed). A click on the Translate button invokes the Yandex translation service and renders the translated text. This latter can now be indicated as output of the recorded interaction process. A click on the Stop button terminates the recording and opens a pop-up window that provides the user with a simple script that can be used to invoke the recorded user interactions. This script is shown in Fig. 13 in the JavaScript console (the string in red) and used inside an `iapi.each` iterator that scans all news articles in the table and allows the invocation of the `iapi.fill_Form` function that mimics the filling of the translation form for each summary found in the table (❼). The final re-render instruction in the JavaScript console renders the retrieved translations (❽), and closing the console brings us to the final mashup already shown in Fig. 4.

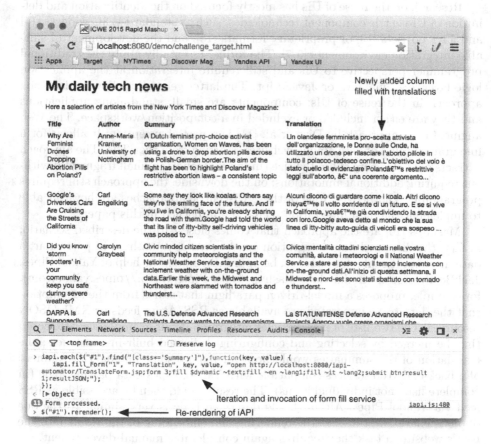

Fig. 13. Iteration over all articles and invocation of the translation form for each summary with final re-rendering of the target iAPI (Color figure online).

The eight described steps showcase how the UI-oriented computing paradigm has been implemented so far for both users and programmers. The video available at http://youtu.be/yEtjIO3oMsI shows the screen cast of the demonstration and provides better insight into the subjective experience of both types of developers.

6   Related Work

The key idea of UI-oriented computing is to interpret standard UI elements – like the ones already in use for the implementation of Web UIs – as constructs to express generic computation logics. Traditionally, computation logic for the Web is expressed either via programming languages, such as Java, Python, PHP, JavaScript, and similar, or via model-driven development formalisms [6]. Orthogonally to these paradigms, Web services [2,12] have emerged over the last decade as one of the most prominent Web technologies that influenced integration on the Web in general. Their focus, however, is on the application logic layer, not the presentation layer (the UIs) of applications.

Research on the reuse of UIs has mostly focused on the identification and definition of UI-centric component technologies, such as standard W3C widgets [14] and Java portlets [13] or proprietary formats [15], and the development of suitable integration environments [5,7]. The former essentially apply the traditional programmer perspective to UIs and still require integration at the application logic layer, e.g., via Java or JavaScript. The latter generally follow a black-box approach in the reuse of UIs: components are small, stand-alone applications and they are either included or excluded in a composition/workspace. The Web augmentation approach by Diaz et al. [11] is a partial exception: it allows for a fine-grained reuse of data among websites, starting from their UIs. The approach extracts data elements of limited size (individual labels or small fragments) without requiring additional annotations; on the downside, the approach still requires programming knowledge. None of these UI-centric approaches are however able to implement the data integration scenario approached in this paper.

Mashups [10] are the approach that comes closest to the described scenario; in fact, the discussed data integration can be seen as a mashup, in particular, a data mashup. It could, for instance, be approached with the help of Yahoo! Pipes, JackBe Presto, or similar data mashup tools. Pipes (http://pipes.yahoo.com), for example, proposes a model-driven paradigm that starts from the assumption that the data to be integrated are available as RSS/Atom feeds or XML/JSON resources. The two lists of news articles integrated in our example scenario could thus be merged by selecting and configuring dedicated built-in constructs; the translation of the summaries would however require some manual development of a back-end Web services compatible with Yahoo! Pipes data passing logic (in complete lists, not individual items). The result would then be accessible as RSS feed via Yahoo! Pipes. Although the described logic is very similar to the one of our scenario, it still lacks the rendering and embedding of the result into the user's website, a task that requires again considerable manual development.

To aid both the extraction of content from HTML markup and the transparent invocation of backend Web services, this paper proposes the use of explicit annotations, similar to microformats (http://microformats.org). If these are not provided natively inside of the markup of a source page (as in the case of the form we annotated for the reuse of the RESTful translation service), the iAPI Annotator provides the necessary means to attach them from the outside to third-party pages (as in the case of the New York Times). The approach does not yet focus on the annotation of data with semantics, as proposed by the Semantic Web initiative [3]. The goal of the annotations in this work is to provide immediate functional benefits to the consumers of data: annotations in fact allow the injection of graphical controls that enable the visual UIC paradigm.

7 Discussion and Future Work

The demo showcased in the context of the Rapid Mashup Challenge and described in this paper is the development of a simple data mashup following a UI-oriented computing approach. The idea of the approach is to leverage on the graphical UIs of applications as programming artifacts, to extend them with additional, programming-specific controls, and to allow developers (both common users and programmers) to express data integration operations interactively inside the browser without having to write any line of program code. The idea of UI-oriented computing and interactive APIs is still in its infancy. Yet, the demo – although apparently simple – showed a data integration scenario that is not trivial in general but that was solved in a fashion that does not require programming skills (the first part of the demo) or manually programming low-level interactions with Web services or data extractors (second part of the demo). The benefits of the approach therefore span from common users to skilled programmers.

There are however still some limitations that come with the showcased implementation of the UI-oriented computing infrastructure and the iAPI editor:

- The current implementation of the editor does not yet support the visual specification of iterators and the reuse of recorded user interactions for the automation of forms. We turned this shortcoming in the demo into an advantage and used it to also showcase how programmers can leverage on the proposed paradigm. This was possible thanks to the ready implementation of the respective functionality in the `iapi` JavaScript library. The next step is however making the these features available also to regular users through the interactive iAPI editor.
- The interaction paradigm proposed in this paper and the demonstration to derive programming intentions from user interactions is a best-effort development. We did not yet have time to study different types of interpretations (e.g., whether a drag and drop action better represents a data fetching action or a layout action) or different interaction paradigms (e.g., without drag and drop actions, with contextual menus that can be opened with a right-click, voice interactions, etc.). However, the current implementation of the described software infrastructure already supports the independent development of different editors on top of the runtime environment, which will ease these kinds of investigations in future developments.

– The annotation format proposed so far to equip UIs with interactive programming capabilities, the interactive APIs, does not leverage on any form of semantic knowledge. The format is inspired by the microformats 2 proposal (http://microformats.org/) and provides syntactic cues for the runtime environment only. We are aware that especially targeting end users without specific programming skills may require better assistance mechanism, able to provide them with as much aid as possible. Doing so may require using also semantic annotations, e.g., in order to automate some data integration tasks (most notably, data disambiguations).

– The UI-oriented computing features supported so far are mostly focused on data integration tasks, with the exception of the user interaction recorder that allows interpreting standard HTML forms as reusable pieces of business logic. The idea of UI-oriented computing is however much broader and comprises also use cases for cloning complete UI widgets (markup, styles and functionality), automating short-living and long-living processes (e.g., the parametric execution of repeated navigation actions), and the establishment of communications among integrated widgets or UI elements. These advanced use cases are part of our future work.

As these considerations point out, UI-oriented computing is not a pure engineering problem only. Identifying the right set of operations and use cases that make sense in a UI-only context, understanding how to best interpret user intentions, designing effective interaction paradigms, etc. are all HCI challenges that need good answers on their own. Of course, the engineering of the necessary software support inside and outside of the browser requires profound software engineering and Web development skills. The challenge of the proposed idea is finding the right answers in both areas and to bring them together profitably. The final vision of iAPIs and UI-oriented computing is proposing an alternative to the current interpretation that programming is only for skilled programmers that can only be achieved by means of abstractions and constructs that only programmers are familiar with and can master. That is, the vision is to make "programming" accessible to an increasingly wider area of "developers."

What makes us confident about the potential success of UI-oriented computing is that, although it's final vision targets non-programmers, it also immediately provides tangible benefits the programmers: The deployment of iAPIs is contextual to the deployment of their host application, and they do not require separate deployment or maintenance (like, for instance, the RSS feeds published by the New York Times in parallel to the main Web site). The documentation of iAPIs comes for free; the UI and the injected graphical controls already tell everything about them. The retrieval of iAPIs does not ask for new infrastructure or query paradigms; since iAPIs are an integral part of the Surface Web, it is enough to query for desired data or functionality via common Web search; if Google indexes a Web site, its iAPIs are indexed too.

The iAPI microformat is maintained via the W3C Interactive APIs Community Group (http://www.w3.org/community/interative-apis), the browser extension on https://github.com/floriandanielit/interactive-apis.

References

1. Abdelnur, A., Hepper, S.: Java Portlet Specification, Version 1.0. Technical Report JSR 168, Sun Microsystems Inc., October 2003. http://download.oracle.com/otndocs/jcp/PORTLET_1.0-FR-SPEC-G-F/

2. Alonso, G., Casati, F., Kuno, H., Machiraju, V.: Web Services: Concepts, Architectures, and Applications. Springer, Heidelberg (2003)

3. Berners-Lee, T., Hendler, J., Lassila, O.: The semantic web. Sci. Am. **284**(5), 34–43 (2001)

4. Caceres, M.: Packaged web apps (widgets) - packaging and xml configuration, 2nd edn. W3C Recommendation (2012)

5. Cappiello, C., Matera, M., Picozzi, M., Sprega, G., Barbagallo, D., Francalanci, C.: DashMash: a mashup environment for end user development. In: Auer, S., Díaz, O., Papadopoulos, G.A. (eds.) ICWE 2011. LNCS, vol. 6757, pp. 152–166. Springer, Heidelberg (2011)

6. Ceri, S., Fraternali, P., Bongio, A., Brambilla, M., Comai, S., Matera, M.: Designing Data-Intensive Web Applications. Morgan Kauffmann, San Francisco (2002)

7. Chudnovskyy, O., Nestler, T., Gaedke, M., Daniel, F., Fernández-Villamor, J.I., Chepegin, V.I., Fornas, J.A., Wilson, S., Kögler, C., Chang, H.: End-user-oriented telco mashups: the OMELETTE approach. In: WWW 2012 (Companion Volume), pp. 235–238 (2012)

8. Daniel, F.: Live, personal data integration through UI-oriented computing. In: Cimiano, P., Frasincar, F., Houben, G.-J., Schwabe, D. (eds.) ICWE 2015. LNCS, vol. 9114, pp. 479–497. Springer, Heidelberg (2015)

9. Daniel, F., Furlan, A.: The interactive API (iAPI). In: Sheng, Q.Z., Kjeldskov, J. (eds.) ICWE 2013 Workshops. LNCS, vol. 8295, pp. 3–15. Springer, Heidelberg (2013)

10. Daniel, F., Matera, M.: Mashups: Concepts, Models and Architectures. Springer, Heidelberg (2014)

11. Díaz, O., Arellano, C., Azanza, M.: A language for end-user web augmentation: caring for producers and consumers alike. ACM Trans. Web **7**(2), 9:1–9:51 (2013)

12. Fielding, R.: Architectural styles and the design of network-based software architectures. Ph.D. Dissertation, University of California, Irvine (2007)

13. Hepper, S.: Java Portlet Specification, Version 2.0, Early Draft. Technical Report JSR 286, IBM Corp., July 2006. http://download.oracle.com/otndocs/jcp/portlet-2.0-edr-oth-JSpec/

14. Web Application Working Group. Widgets Family of Specifications. Technical report, W3C, May 2012. http://www.w3.org/2008/webapps/wiki/WidgetSpecs

15. Yu, J., Benatallah, B., Saint-Paul, R., Casati, F., Daniel, F., Matera, M.: A framework for rapid integration of presentation components. In: WWW 2007, pp. 923–932 (2007)

SmartComposition: Extending Web Applications to Multi-screen Mashups

Michael Krug[✉], Fabian Wiedemann, and Martin Gaedke

Technische Universität Chemnitz, Chemnitz, Germany
{michael.krug,fabian.wiedemann,martin.gaedke}@informatik.tu-chemnitz.de

Abstract. The overall objective of UI mashups is to enable non-experts to create rich web applications. While current approaches focus on creating UI mashups running on a single screen, we propose SmartComposition to enable local developers to create multi-screen mashups. We present our enhanced SmartComponents, which are based on the latest developments of the family of W3C standards called "Web Components", as part of our SmartComposition approach. SmartComponents provide loosely coupling and support both single- and multi-device usage scenarios by extending Web Components with dedicated communication and synchronization features. We support multiple types of Smart-Components, not limiting them to user interface components. In contrast to other approaches, SmartComponents are independent, encapsulated, configurable and programmable, which ensures hassle-free reuse in any HTML5 web application. SmartComposition provides an event-based communication infrastructure which enables inter-component communication as well as message exchange across multiple screens utilizing a WebSocket-based synchronization service.

Keywords: Component-based web engineering · Web components · Distributed multi-device web applications · Web application development · Composition · Reusable components · Multi-screen mashup · HTML5

1 Introduction

Within the last years, the amount of tools for creating user interface mashups (UI mashups) significantly increased. The overall objective of UI mashups is to enable non-experts to create rich web applications [2]. For solving complex tasks an UI mashup consists of several components that offer a limited functionality and are combined and aggregated. While other approaches for creating UI mashups focus on automatic or semi-automatic mashup creation and deployment to desktop as well as mobile screens, our approach eases the creation of UI mashups that run distributed across several screens, so called multi-screen mashups.

The purpose of SmartComposition is to enable local developers to create multi-screen mashups. We assume that a local developer is familiar with basic web technologies, such as HTML5 and CSS [1]. Thus, our approach is based on these technologies and does not require advanced knowledge of JavaScript. Furthermore,

© Springer International Publishing Switzerland 2016
F. Daniel and C. Pautasso (Eds.): RMC 2015, CCIS 591, pp. 50–62, 2016.
DOI: 10.1007/978-3-319-28727-0_4

we want to achieve a high level of reuse of the developed components. This requires loosely coupling and a suitable communication infrastructure to minimize the overhead when integrating them. For enhancing existing web applications to multi screen mashups, SmartComposition needs to be easily integrable.

In the last years, with the rapid advancement of JavaScript, a lot of client-side components were provided as JavaScript libraries or snippets. Mostly, their functionality is added to standard HTML elements by calling special JavaScript functions that extents them. Those elements are then used as containers to host more dynamically created HTML elements. Common examples would be image slideshows, lightboxes, map sections or enhanced user interface components. Well known libraries that support such components are e.g., jQuery and Dojo.

We observed several limitations and problems using those approaches: First of all, those components cannot be used directly in the HTML code. A placeholder element has to be added to the document on which some JavaScript code is applied. Secondly, such solutions require an advanced knowledge of JavaScript and cumbersome configuration and instantiation is needed. Furthermore, since the components are created in the same DOM (Document Object Model) tree as the host document, a high risk of conflicts with existing elements and style definitions is present.

Most of the currently existing JavaScript components are designed to work separately. A mashup-like scenario, where the composition of multiple components that work together forms a new application, is not tackled. In such scenarios a uniform way to exchange data between components is required. Former research dealt with the integration of inter-widget communication in existing widgets approaches, like W3C or OpenSocial Widgets [7]. Unfortunately, these widget types need to be deployed and hosted in portal environments like Apache Rave or Apache Shindig.

The rest of this paper is organized as follows: First, we outline the context and goals of the SmartComposition approach. In the next chapter, we present related work. Section 4 will describe the SmartComposition approach itself. In Sect. 5 the requested feature checklist is provided. Finally, we describe our preparation for the mashup challenge, the demonstration itself and conclude our paper.

2   Context and Goals of the SmartComposition Approach

The focus of our SmartComposition approach is the client-side composition with an emphasis on user-interface components. To make our approach stand out from other solutions, we set the goal to support and ease the development of multi-screen capable web applications. We want to eliminate the requirement of many other approaches that need a dedicated runtime environment and enable usage in any standard HTML5 website or application. Therefore, we aim to use only client-side JavaScript and standard Web technologies. We do not want to limit the types of components in our approach. Thus, our solution should enable the development and usage of UI as well as data or logic components. A combination of all three types should also be possible. In contrast to existing UI mashup approaches, where components are mostly called *widgets*, we always use the term *component*. This is justified by not limiting our component types to user interface elements. To ease the development of multi-screen capable web applications, we want to provide not only inter-component communication but also a easy to integrate multi-device message exchange functionality.

How we reached our goals will be presented in the following chapters, after we state related approaches for client-side component-based web development.

3 Related Work

Since we especially focus on the component technologies for creating mashups by composition, we will state related work in the field of component technologies in the Web.

jQuery[1] provides a plugin system that enables developers to create extended HTML elements. In most cases the instantiation and configuration is done by selecting the desired element and applying the provided plugin constructor to it. Elements are inserted in the document's DOM and therefore are not encapsulated. Communication features are not included.

Dojo[2] focuses on a more comprehensive approach and provides a UI library called Dijit. Dijit is a widget system layered on top of Dojo. Dojo widgets are instantiated and configured using the "data-dojo-type" and "data-dojo-props" attributes in the HTML markup. The template content in inserted directly in the document's DOM what increases the risk for conflicts. Dojo provides a topic-based publish/subscribe mechanism for communication purposes.

W3C Widgets[3] (also called Packaged Web Apps) and OpenSocial Widgets[4] are open web standards. Since they need to be executed in special platform environments, such as Apache Rave[5] or Apache Shindig[6], the acceptance and usage is limited. They provide encapsulation by running in iFrames and can exploit inter-widget-communication features for composing applications like mashups. The integration of OpenAjax Hub[7] into Apache Rave is an approach to achieve communication between those widgets. The DireWolf framework [4] is one solution that integrates multi-device communication into the Apache Shindig platform.

Another approach is MultiMasher [3]. MultiMasher is a visual tool for multi-device mashups using a direct manipulation interface where a user can select existing UI elements and send them to connected devices. There, the elements will be mashed up with the content that has been sent. Thus, in contrast to the widget approaches, MultiMasher does not support separated components but relies on existing UI elements.

---

[1] http://jquery.com.
[2] http://dojotoolkit.org.
[3] http://www.w3.org/TR/widgets/.
[4] http://opensocial.atlassian.net/wiki/display/OSD/Specs.
[5] http://rave.apache.org/.
[6] http://shindig.apache.org/.
[7] http://www.openajax.org/member/wiki/OpenAjax_Hub_2.0_Specification.

4 The SmartComposition Approach

The SmartComposition approach is based on the idea of creating mashups by composing loosely coupled components using standard web technologies. In [6], Krug et al. proposed a component-based architecture for multi-screen web applications. We advance the presented ideas by using the *Web Components* technologies for defining and implementing SmartComponents.

We propose a uniform way of defining, implementing and composing loosely coupled independent components by using the new set of W3C standards called *Web Components*. Thus, we support developers in handling those new technologies by providing an extended version of the Polymer framework[8] that wraps the creation of Web Components in an easy-to-use declarative syntax and is enriched with new communication features based on an event-driven architecture. Additionally, we present an optional messaging service that seamlessly integrates into an application developed with the SmartComposition approach and provides message exchange between multiple devices.

The major benefit of using the proposed technologies for creating modern widgets is that no dedicated portal software is needed to host such composed applications. This enables the integration of SmartComponents into common content management systems like WordPress, Drupal or Joomla, as well as in any other HTML5 based website.

To make multi-screen mashup applications more interactive, SmartComponents can be configured to be easily movable by drag-and-drop. Additionally, SmartComponents can also be moved to other connected screens with their state preserved. SmartComponents are stateful DOM objects and provide script interfaces. Thus, developers are able to influence the behavior of the used components on runtime with standard HTML5 DOM methods. SmartComponents can be added, removed and reconfigured at any time. By making SmartComponents available as HTML elements, users that are familiar with HTML but do not have knowledge in programming are also able to create mashups.

In the following section we will guide through the structure of SmartComponents and their technological background.

4.1 Structure of SmartComponents

SmartComponents exploit a set of new W3C technologies called *Web Components*, consisting of *Templates, Shadow DOM, Custom Elements* and *HTML Imports*. The first technology called *Templates* (http://w3.org/TR/html5/scripting-1.html) defines chunks of markup that are inert but can be activated for use later. That means, the content of the template element is parsed by the parser, but it is inactive and not rendered. Within the `<template>` tags normal HTML markup is used to describe the structure of the components static content. When creating the component, the template's content is copied to an adjunct DOM tree called *Shadow DOM* (http://w3.org/TR/shadow-dom/). The *Shadow DOM* is the second

---

[8] http://www.polymer-project.org.

new W3C standard in the set of *Web Components*. This adjunct tree of DOM nodes can be associated with an element, but does not appear as a child node of the element. Instead, the subtree forms its own scope. Due to the different scope of the Shadow DOM, the styles, names or IDs of elements in the root document do not interfere with the definitions in the component.

The template is followed by an optional style section, where the look of the component's content can be defined. Existing style sheet definitions can be reused by including the CSS @import statement. To address the custom element that is hosting the component's content, the new pseudo-class :host is provided. Due to the previously mentioned scoping, the developer has not to worry about conflicting style definitions, class names or IDs.

New SmartComponents are defined using a declarative syntax provided by the Polymer framework. An example definition file for a SmartComponent is shown in Listing 1.

```
<dom−module id=" wikipedia−extract ">
  <style>
    :host { display: inline−block; }
  </style>
  <template>
    <div id=" container "></div>
  </template>
  <script>
    Polymer({
      is: 'wikipedia−extract ',
      behaviors: [Polymer.SmartComponentBehavior],
      properties: {
        query: {
          type: String ,
          reflectToAttribute: true ,
          observer: 'queryChanged '
        }
      },
      queryChanged: function () {
        // Request to fetch data from Wikipedia
      },
      attached: function () {
        this.subscribe ('wiki ', this.queryReceived );
      },
      detached: function () {
        this.unsubscribe ('wiki ', this.queryReceived );
      },
      queryReceived: function (message) {
        this.query = message.data;
      }
    });
  </script>
</dom−module>
```

Listing 1. Definition file of a SmartComponent

This declarative description handles all necessary actions to create a custom element and setting up event bindings. A developer can define any number of properties that can be configured with type settings, observer functions and e.g. reflection to attributes. By using the *behaviors* property to inject our *Smart-ComponentBehavior*, we can provide our later described extensions for inter-component communication without modifying the Polymer framework itself. This supports the maintainability of both our extension and the framework.

SmartComponents are new types of DOM elements that can be defined by developers. They are stateful DOM objects and provide script interfaces. New components can be easily integrated in a website by using *HTML Imports* (http://w3.org/TR/html-imports/). The import statement uses the <link> tag to load external definition files (see Listing 2). The new custom element tag can be instantly used in the HTML markup after importing the component resource file. SmartComponents are registered as new HTML elements. Thus, they can be used them in the same way as other standard elements. The usage requires no knowledge of JavaScript. Configuration is possible through attributes or child elements.

```
<html>
<head>
  <link rel="import" href="smart-component.html">
</head>
<body>
  <smart-component some-attr="some-value"></smart-component>
</body>
</html>
```

Listing 2. Usage of SmartComponents in HTML5 websites

In the following section we will describe the communication aspect we integrated into the components of the SmartComposition approach.

4.2   Inter-Component Communication

Loosely coupling of components is important to ensure reuse and enable new compositions. To support message exchange between SmartComponents we therefore propose an event-driven communication channel using a topic-based publish/subscribe mechanism. Figure 1 provides a simplified overview of the inter-component and inter-device communication architecture of the SmartComposition approach.

Components can consume and produce events described by a topic and the attached data. The publish/subscribe message bus is implemented using the JavaScript's native eventing system. Messages are sent using a custom event and received by adding an event listener for that custom event. The payload can be structured objects or simple values.

As it is displayed in Listing 1, the *subscribe* method should be called within the life-cycle event *attached*, which means when the component is added to the DOM.

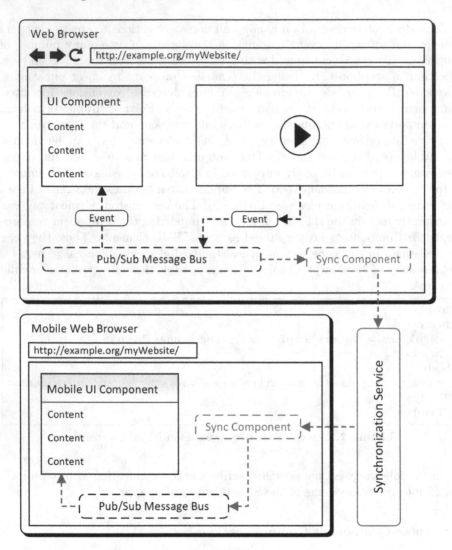

Fig. 1. Simplified inter-component and inter-device communication architecture

But this is not a limitation. In fact, it can be called anytime after attaching. To stop the SmartComponent from consuming events after it is removed from the DOM, the *unsubscribe* method should be called within the *detached* life-cycle event. A Smart-Component can have any number of subscriptions to any topic. Messages can be sent using a *publish(topic, data)* method that is available in the SmartComponent context. All communication functionality is injected using the *behaviors* property and contained in our implemented *SmartComponentBehavior*.

By employing this eventing system and by giving the message a predefined structure, containing the topic and the data, we achieve a topic-based and event-driven communication channel. Without blocking the user interface, we ensure high performant and low latency communication by relying on JavaScript's native event system.

In the following section we show how inter-component communication is extended for multi-device usage.

4.3 Inter-Device Communication

By providing a WebSocket-based synchronization service, we enable developers to easily create multi-device-capable web applications. Our approach proposes a stand-alone solution with no dependencies and side-effects on other components. The solution consists of a synchronization server and a client-side messaging service. The client-side component is also implemented as SmartComponent that captures all events transmitted on the previously described publish/subscribe message bus and sends them to the server-side component. When the client-side component receives a message from the server, it sends it back to the local message bus where the components will be notified.

We are utilizing the WebSocket protocol (https://tools.ietf.org/html/rfc6455) for the client-server communication. This provides us with a full-duplex, low-latency communication channel based on standard web technologies. The server-side component is implemented as a WebSocket server using Node.js.

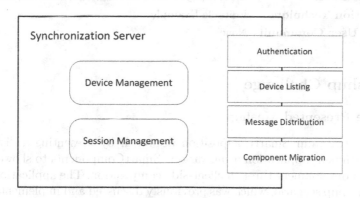

Fig. 2. Basic functionality of the synchronization server

The WebSocket server (see Fig. 2) provides functionality for a set of message types (authentication, clients, ping, data) and can easily be extended. Received messages are analyzed and broadcast to groups (*sessions*) of connected devices. We define the term *connected devices* as: devices with the same synchronization endpoint that share the same session identifier, i.e. context. The session identifier enables the usage of one synchronization endpoints for multiple application contexts. The basic functionality is that messages are only distributed to devices within the same session. Another task of the server-side component is the management of connected devices. On connection, each device will get an up-to-date list of connected devices with their details (name, type, identifier). This list is also updated and distributed if a client connects, disconnects or changes its details.

One major advantage of our synchronization approach is that no reconfiguration of existing components is necessary for multi-device communication. Since the messaging service is working like a hook, all messages sent by the Smart-Components are captured without changing the code or configuration.

5   Feature Checklist

Mashup Type	Hybrid mashups
Component Types	Data components
	Logic components
	UI components
Runtime Location	Both Client and Server
Integration Logic	Choreographed integration
Instantiation Lifecycle	Short-living
Targeted End-User	Local Developers
Automation Degree	Manual
Liveness Level	Level 4 (Dynamic Modificationof Running Mashup)
Interaction Technique	Editable Example
Online User Community	None

6   Mashup Challenge

6.1   The Presented Mashup

We demonstrate our SmartComposition approach by presenting a distributed media enrichment application using various SmartComponents to showcase web application development through client-side composition. The application implements a mashup scenario, which was previously discussed and implemented without the usage of *Web Components* in [5]. One possible resulting mashup can be seen in Fig. 3.

To create an application by composition, multiple SmartComponents can be imported and inserted into an HTML website as it is displayed in Listing 3.

We start our mashup with an empty web page that has an option to add new components to the application. Using the New York Times news feed component as the starting point, we add more and more components that work together to form a new interactive experience. For a detailed description of the mashup components and how they work together see Sect. 6.3.

To proof the multi-device capabilities of our solution, we show that Smart-Components can display different kinds of information synchronized on multiple devices, and that they can even be moved between devices. Our demos can be

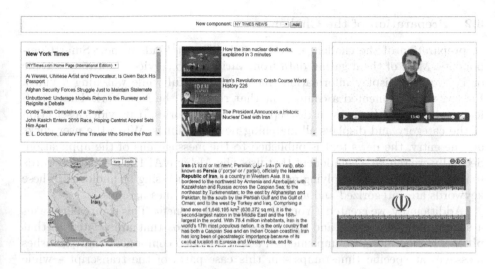

Fig. 3. Screenshot of the presented mashup

used in any modern web browser without the installation of additional software. Not all technologies we are using are currently implemented in all browsers as most of them are still W3C working drafts. By optionally using the webcompo-nent.js polyfills (http://webcomponents.org/polyfills/), SmartComponents are also enabled in web browsers that lack native support.

Online Demonstration:
http://vsr-demo.informatik.tu-chemnitz.de/smartcomposition/icwe2015/

```html
<html>
  <head>
    <link rel="import" href="nytimes-news-component.html">
    <link rel="import" href="semantic-extraction-component.html">
    ...
  </head>
  <body>
    <nytimes-news></nytimes-news>
    <semantic-extraction></semantic-extraction>
    <youtube-search query="Iran"></youtube-search>
    <smart-video></smart-video>
    <google-geocoder address="Iran"></google-geocoder>
    <google-map lat="51" lng="12" zoom="12"></google-map>
    <twitter-tweets query="Iran"></twitter-tweets>
    <wikipedia-extract query="Iran"></wikipedia-extract>
    <google-images query="Iran"></google-images>
  </body>
</html>
```

Listing 3. Application development by composition

6.2 Preparation of the Challenge

In preparation of the challenge, we created different kinds of new SmartComponents. Most of them gather data from various web services regarding a topic or keyword to display information that can be useful while watching a video. Firstly, we implemented a component that retrieves the New York Times RSS feed and extracts the news entries separated by categories. It provides a selection of the category and displays all matching news headlines. When the user clicks on one entry, the news text is published to the message bus of the application. Secondly, we reused a component that uses the AlchemyAPI to extract keywords (entities) from text by applying natural language processing technologies. These keywords are categorized and again published to our message bus.

Additionally, we created a YouTube search component. This component takes a search phrase as input and displays a list of videos that are related to that phrase. Furthermore, we implemented a special video component that publishes messages at specific timestamps - in this case parts of the transcript - while playing a video. This is done by exploiting the TextTrack-API and an attached VTT subtitles file containing time-based metadata. The video component works with local videos as input as well as with YouTube URLs that are automatically resolved. To visualize information about different entities, we implemented components that catch data from web sources, like Twitter, Google Maps, Images and Wikipedia. A drawback that needs to mentioned is that the topic names and data formats of connected components have to be known by the developers.

6.3 The Demo Flow

In general, the first source of information can be any component. In our specific demonstration, we use the New York Times news feed as an entry point. New components can be easily added to the application by either stating them in the markup or adding them dynamically using the given select box and button. When the user clicks on one of the displayed news headline entries, the component publishes the corresponding news text. By adding the semantic extraction component, the mashup is able to obtain different entities from published text content. They are annotated with categories and can be used by other components to retrieve related information. If there is e.g., an entity categorized as *location*, the Google Maps Geocoder component is using the entity to convert it to geographical coordinates that can be again consumed by the Google Maps component to display this place on a map. Furthermore, entities of the type *person* can be e.g., visualized by the Google Images or Wikipedia component. To make the mashup more interactive, not only the news feed is used as information source. The gathered entities are also used by the YouTube search component to retrieve related videos with subtitles. If the user clicks on one of the listed videos, it will be passed to the video component that is able to play the video and at the same time publish time-based metadata. The metadata - in this case the transcript - is also used for semantic extraction and will trigger the display of different kind of information visualizations. An example message flow can be seen in Fig. 4.

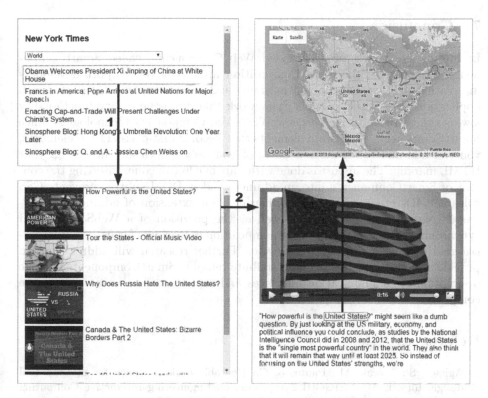

Fig. 4. Message flow of an example mashup

The extension of the mashup to use multi-device communication is straightforward. First of all, a synchronization server has to be set up, which is a Node.js WebSocket server. Additionally, the messaging service has to be included in the web application and configured with the endpoint address as displayed in Listing 4.

```
<link  rel="import" href="MessagingService.html">

<messaging−service
 endpoint="http://example.org:1234" session="SessionID">
</messaging−service>
```

Listing 4. Code snippet of the messaging-service

Any reconfiguration or even altering of code of existing SmartComponents is not necessary. All published events will now be synchronized between multiple connected devices. Applying it to the mashup application, it then can be used on different devices in parallel with synchronized state without touching the code of the components. Thus, the user can display e.g., the Google Map on his mobile device while watching the video on his laptop.

7   Conclusion

In this paper we presented extended Web Components, called SmartComponents, as a part of the SmartComposition approach. We support developers in creating multi-screen-enabled mashups and other complex, distributed web applications. Using the Polymer framework that wraps necessary functionality lowers the barrier of using the new W3C Web Components technologies. Since SmartComponents are custom elements that become first-class HTML elements, you can add and configure new parts of you web application directly in your HTML markup. The import is done with only one line of code. Inserting the content of SmartComponents into an adjunct shadow DOM subtree prevents CSS rules and IDs of elements from conflicting. Our extension of adding an event-based communication channel as well as the provision of a WebSocket-based synchronization service enables the composition of mashups for usage across distributed platforms and multiple devices. Further research will address how to provide a repository to store and distribute reusable SmartComponents and the description of communication interfaces and topic names to ensure hassle-free composition of SmartComponents.

References

1. Aghaee, S., Nowak, M., Pautasso, C.: Reusable decision space for mashup tool design. In: 4th ACM SIGCHI Symposium on Engineering Interactive Computing Systems, pp. 211–220, Copenhagen, Denmark, June 2012
2. Chudnovskyy, O., Fischer, C., Gaedke, M., Pietschmann, S.: Inter-widget communication by demonstration in user interface mashups. In: Daniel, F., Dolog, P., Li, Q. (eds.) ICWE 2013. LNCS, vol. 7977, pp. 502–505. Springer, Heidelberg (2013)
3. Husmann, M., Nebeling, M., Norrie, M.C.: Multimasher: a visual tool for multi-device mashups. In: Sheng, Q.Z., Kjeldskov, J. (eds.) ICWE Workshops 2013. LNCS, vol. 8295, pp. 27–38. Springer, Heidelberg (2013)
4. Kovachev, D., Renzel, D., Nicolaescu, P., Klamma, R.: Direwolf - distributing and migrating user interfaces for widget-based web applications. In: Daniel, F., Dolog, P., Li, Q. (eds.) ICWE 2013. LNCS, vol. 7977, pp. 99–113. Springer, Heidelberg (2013)
5. Krug, M., Wiedemann, F., Gaedke, M.: Enhancing media enrichment by semantic extraction. In: Proceedings of the Companion Publication of the 23rd International Conference on World Wide Web Companion, WWW Companion 2014, pp. 111–114. International World Wide Web Conferences Steering Committee (2014)
6. Krug, M., Wiedemann, F., Gaedke, M.: Smartcomposition: a component-based approach for creating multi-screen mashups. In: Casteleyn, S., Rossi, G., Winckler, M. (eds.) ICWE 2014. LNCS, vol. 8541, pp. 236–253. Springer, Heidelberg (2014)
7. Wilson, S., Daniel, F., Jugel, U., Soi, S.: Orchestrated user interface mashups using W3C widgets. In: Harth, A., Koch, N. (eds.) ICWE 2011. LNCS, vol. 7059, pp. 49–61. Springer, Heidelberg (2012)

EFESTO: A Platform for the End-User Development of Interactive Workspaces for Data Exploration

Giuseppe Desolda[1]([✉]), Carmelo Ardito[1], and Maristella Matera[2]

[1] Dipartimento di Informatica, Università degli Studi di Bari Aldo Moro,
Via Orabona, 4, 70125 Bari, Italy
{giuseppe.desolda, carmelo.ardito}@uniba.it
[2] Dipartimento di Elettronica, Informazione e Bioingegneria,
Politecnico di Milano, Piazza Leonardo da Vinci, 32, 20134 Milan, Italy
maristella.matera@polimi.it

Abstract. This paper illustrates EFESTO, a mashup platform designed to enable end users to explore information by creating interactive workspaces. Within a Web composition environment, end users dynamically create "live mashups" where relevant information, extracted from heterogeneous data sources - including the Linked Open Data – is integrated according to visually defined queries. Visualizations of the resulting data sets can be flexibly shaped-up at runtime. Functions, exposed by local or remote services, also allow users to manipulate the resulting data depending on their situational needs. With respect to other mashup platforms, EFESTO privileges visual composition paradigms that accommodate the end-user mental model for a lightweight data integration within Web workspaces.

Keywords: Mashups · Web composition environments · Data integration

1 Introduction

Mashups are data-centric applications that can be created by composing heterogeneous resources [1]. They are considered a solution for supporting data exploration processes that exceed one-time interactions and allow users to progressively seek for information. As studied in [2], typically users invoke general-purpose search engines and/or specialized verticals, and then use "their brain" (or suitable cognitive aids, e.g., annotations or clipboards) for remembering results to be used next. Mashups solve (at least partially) these limitations, as they try to accommodate users' needs for data integration within personal, ad-hoc created workspaces.

Despite these advantages, some factors still prevent a wider use of the mashup paradigm in real contexts, especially by users who are not experts in programming. While mashups have been identified as a useful mean for application development by the end users [1], so far the research on mashups has largely focused on the enabling integration technologies and standards, with limited attention on easing the mashup development process - in many cases mashup creation still involves the manual programming of

© Springer International Publishing Switzerland 2016
F. Daniel and C. Pautasso (Eds.): RMC 2015, CCIS 591, pp. 63–81, 2016.
DOI: 10.1007/978-3-319-28727-0_5

service integration. Some user-centric studies [3] also found that, although the most prominent platforms (e.g., Yahoo!Pipes) tried to simplify mashup development, they are still difficult to use by non-technical users, who encounter difficulties with the adopted composition languages [4]. Besides the complexity of the composition paradigm [5], the active interaction with the retrieved data, by means of exploration and manipulation actions, is hardly supported.

With the intent of overcoming the limitations identified in literature, we defined EFESTO (EFesto End uSer composition plaTfOrm), a platform for the End-User Development of mashups. Efesto was a god of the Greek mythology, who realized magnificent magic arms for other Greek gods and heroes. Analogously, the EFESTO platform aims to put in the hands of end users powerful tools to accomplish their tasks. Our platform, in fact, is characterized by a paradigm for the exploration and composition of heterogeneous data sources that tries to accommodate the end-user mental model for a lightweight data integration within Web workspaces. The paradigm was designed taking into account the results of some elicitation studies aimed to identify the end-user mental model for service composition [5, 6]. It was also validated during two field studies in specific application domains, namely Cultural Heritage [5] and Technology Enhanced Learning [7]. Besides helping us assess the elicited mental model, these studies also highlighted new (unexpected) requirements. Among the most important ones, the users expressed the need to manipulate, in a more powerful way, data extracted from services, and the possibility to satisfy more complex information needs by gathering data from the entire Web - not only from pre-packaged components. To overcome these drawbacks, the most recent version of EFESTO offers: *(i)* visual mechanisms to integrate data retrieved from different data sources; *(ii)* a new "polymorphic" data source model that, by exploiting the Linked Open Data (LOD) cloud, enables the access to "mutable" information depending on the situational needs expressed in the mashup under construction; *(iii)* a set of tools to organize, visualize and manipulate extracted data according to specific functions. This new version of the platform is available online at the address: http://efesto.ddns.net/.

This paper illustrates EFESTO with a specific focus on the features presented and discussed during the ICWE 2015 Rapid Mashup Challenge. In particular, Sect. 2 presents, by means of a scenario, the composition paradigm implemented in our mashup platform and also illustrates the sequence of composition steps presented at the challenge. Section 3 describes the platform architecture and in particular the mechanisms supporting the visual construction of live mashups and the way the platform invokes and integrates heterogeneous services, including LOD data sources. Section 4 discusses the level of maturity of our platform, by illustrating how EFESTO has been customized, adopted and evaluated in specific application domains. Section 5 emphasizes the peculiarities of EFESTO by comparing it with other mashup platforms. Section 6 reports how we prepared for the Rapid Mashup Challenge. Section 7 concludes the paper and outlines our current and future work.

2 The EFESTO Composition Paradigm

To illustrate the main features of EFESTO, we now introduce a usage scenario that recalls the live demo given during the ICWE 2015 rapid mashup challenge[1].

Let us consider an end user, Michael, who is going to organize his summer holidays. Michael has not yet decided where to go between London and Madrid but, regardless the destination, he would like to attend a concert during his holidays. For this reason, Michael uses EFESTO to retrieve and integrate various information (i.e., to create mashups) about music events. Michael starts looking for pertinent services among those registered in the platform. A **wizard procedure** guides him to make a selection from a popup window where services are classified by category (e.g., videos, photos, music, social). Michael selects *SongKick*, a service that provides information on music events given an artist name. He also selects a map *UI template* for displaying the retrieved information. The aim of Michael's activities in the EFESTO workspace is indeed to create some widgets, called *UI components* [8], that visually render, in a chosen format, data extracted from selected data sources. As SongKick data are geo-localized, Michael decides to visualize the retrieved data on a map.

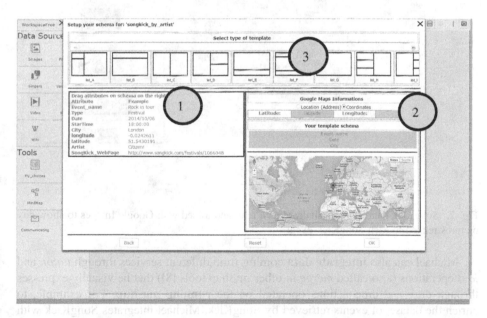

Fig. 1. Mapping between the SongKick data attributes and UI template fields (Color figure online)

As shown in Fig. 1 (circle #1), the SongKick data attributes are visualized in a panel on the left. To make the attributes understandable by the user, the system also shows some example values. First, Michael drags and drops the *latitude* and *longitude*

---

[1] The video that faithfully reports the live demo is available at https://youtu.be/bBG5O266y4g.

SongKick attributes into the related fields in the map UI template (Fig. 1, circle #2). Then he chooses a table UI template with three items in column (Fig. 1, circle #3) for visualizing, when required, some additional details about a musical event. He selects and drops the desired attributes in the fields of the table template (highlighted in yellow in Fig. 1, circle #2). These actions represent queries on the underlying data sources that will be successively executed to create the mashup data set.

After performing the mapping phase, Michael saves the mashup. Figure 2 reports an example of the created mashup, which is **immediately executed** in the Web browser. By typing "Vasco Rossi" in the search box, the forthcoming events of this singer are visualized as pins on the map.

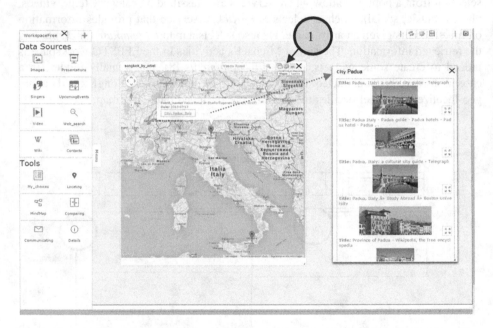

Fig. 2. SongKick data source visualized as a map and joined with Google Images to show city pictures related to each SongKick event

Michael can also **integrate data** coming from different services through *union* and *join* operations (also called *merge* in other mashup tools [8]) that he visually expresses through drag and drop actions operated on the **running mashup**. For example, to enrich the dataset of events retrieved by SongKick, Michael integrates SongKick with *Last.fm*, thus exploiting the union operation. In particular, he acts directly on the SongKick UI component previously created by clicking on the gearwheel icon in the toolbar (pointed by the circle #1 in Fig. 2) and choosing the "Add results from new source" menu item. A wizard procedure now guides Michael in choosing a new service and in performing a new mapping between the Last.fm attributes and the UI template already used when SongKick was created. The newly created dataset is shown in the same fashion as reported in Fig. 2 but now, when queried with an artist name, the widget visualizes results gathered both from the SongKick and Last.fm services.

Another data integration operation available in EFESTO is the join of different datasets. For example, since SongKick does not provide images of the location where concerts are held, Michael joins the SongKick city attribute with *Google Images*; the city name now becomes the keyword for extracting from Google Images a sequence of related pictures. To perform this operation, Michael clicks on the component gearwheel icon and choses the "Extend results with details" menu item. A new wizard procedure guides him while choosing the service attribute to be extended (*City* in this example), the new data source (Google Images) and how to visualize the Google Images results. From now on, as shown in the right-hand side of Fig. 2, when clicking on the city name in the map info window, another pop-up visualizes the Google Images pictures related to the selected city.

Let us suppose now that, during the interaction with EFESTO, Michael wants to get details about the artists of the music events, such as genre, starting year of activity and artist photo. He does not find any service, among those registered in the platform, that can satisfy this new information need. Thus, he decides to join the SongKick artist attribute with a DBpedia-based *polymorphic data source* [9]. The platform now shows a list of properties related to the musical artist class[2], and Michael creates a new data source based on the properties *genre*, *starting year of activity* and *artist photo*. Henceforward, Michael can find a list of upcoming events in the SongKick component and visualize the additional artist's information, retrieved through the new data source, when clicking on the artist name in SongKick. We call this data source "polymorphic" because, different from pre-registered data sources (e.g., Google Images) that only provide a pre-defined, invariable set of properties, it can enable the access to different information (properties) depending on the attribute in the origin data source it is bound to. For example, if the Michael's join starting point is the SongKick *city* attribute, properties like *borough*, *census*, *year*, *demographics* would be proposed.

Another operation available in EFESTO is the *change of visualization* for a given UI component. Michael, in fact, during the interaction with SongKick, decides to switch from the *map UI template* to the *list UI template* (see the result in Fig. 3, circle #1). To perform this action, he clicks on the gearwheel icon in the SongKick toolbar and choses the *Change visualization* menu item. A visual procedure allows Michael to choose a UI template (a list in this case), and drag and drop the SongKick attributes onto the UI template, as already performed during the SongKick creation.

Until now, Michael has aggregated and composed information according to a paradigm that is similar for some aspects to the ones provided by other mashup platforms [1]. Our field studies, however, revealed that mashups generally lack *data manipulation functions* that can be instead useful to support common tasks [5, 7] and can empower the users to play a more active role than just consuming the finally visualized information. We thus extended EFESTO with a set of tools that, by exploiting functions local to the platform or exposed by remote APIs, provide the possibility to "act" on the extracted contents, for example to collect and save favourites,

---

[2] When a service is registered in the platform, each attribute is automatically annotated with a DBpedia class that is semantically close to the attribute meaning [9]; for example the SongKick *Artist* attribute is annotated with the DBpedia *Musical Artist* class.

to compare items, to plot data items on a map, to inspect full content details, or to arrange items in a mind map to highlight relationships [10]. Coming back to our scenario, as shown in Fig. 3, Michael adds some tools into his workspace, each of them devoted to a particular task. For example, each time Michael drags a SongKick event into the *Map* tool (Fig. 3, circle #3), this item is automatically 'translated' as pin on the map. Another example is the *Comparing* tool (Fig. 3, circle #2) that assists the user in comparing items retrieved by one or more services (SongKick events in Fig. 3). In general, item transitions across different tools determine different organizations and visualizations of data and progressively enable different functions.

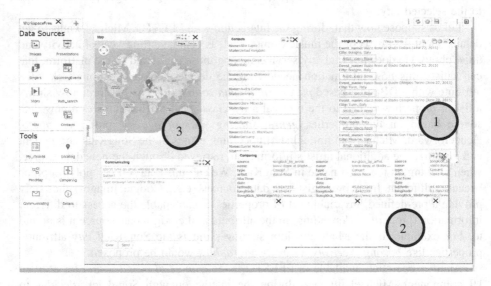

Fig. 3. Use of some tools available in EFESTO to manipulate SongKick data

3   Architecture and Feature Checklist

Figure 4 illustrates the overall organization of EFESTO. The platform supports the composition of **heterogeneous components** (data, UI and logic components) by means of an **orchestration logic** that enables extracting and integrating data and operations provided by different services, mainly to create the so-called **UI components**. A **UI synchronization logic** then allows one to synchronize at the presentation layer the behavior of different UI components. This synchronization is based on an **event-driven paradigm** that couples events generated by source components to operation enacted in target components. The platform thus generates **hybrid mashups** that integrate data and orchestrate functions, and provides structured and coordinated visualizations of the integrated data set and functions.

As already highlighted in the previous section, with respect to other mashup platforms EFESTO is strongly characterized by its interaction layer and, in particular, by its **visual language** that allows the users to create "live" mashups without writing a line of code. The adoption of a visual notation and the liveness of the mashups under construction demand for the definition of an execution logic that is distributed between the platform front-end and back-end and is in charge of interpreting the user composition actions and putting them in action immediately.

Another relevant feature is the capability of generating models (*Workspace Descriptors* and *UI Component Descriptors* as described later in the paper), in a model-driven engineering (MDE) fashion. Models, expressed according to a Domain-Specific Language [5, 8], specify the user composition choices and drive the instantiation of the mashup running code. The MDE paradigm thus enables the deployment of a same mashup on multiple devices, as native execution engines can interpret the same generated models on different target devices. In order to support this execution paradigm, service descriptors are also needed to provide an adequate

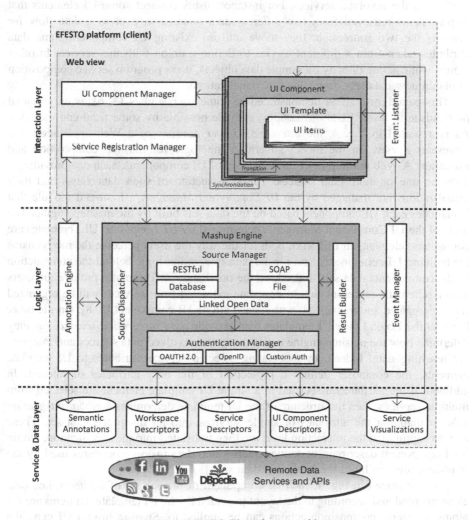

Fig. 4. The EFESTO Three-layers architecture

abstraction layer for invoking and querying services. The rest of this section will illustrate the mechanisms through which different modules, distributed along different layers, interoperate to give life to the EFESTO composition and execution paradigm.

3.1   Interaction Layer

In EFESTO, the *Interaction Layer* provides a kind of key metaphor determining the mashup logic and the overall system behaviour. Operations for mashup composition are indeed expressed by the users through direct manipulation actions on UI elements in charge of rendering data. According to a "programming-by example" paradigm, user actions operated on sample data items extracted from data sources are interpreted as models of queries to be executed on entire data sets and of the orchestration logic to be applied on the involved services. For instance, users connect some UI elements that display items retrieved from two different data sources to express a data flow for merging the two sources; or they move into an existing UI component some data attributes taken from a different service to define a union with this service. In other words, while acting directly on sample data objects, users program service composition to obtain new data sets, functions and visualizations.

This paradigm that, as demonstrated in some user studies [3, 6], is an essential prerequisite to foster EUD of mashups, is made possible by some front-end modules. As represented in Fig. 4, the *Interaction Layer* consists of a Web application that represents a view on the model governing the logic for mashup composition and execution. A Web mashup in EFESTO is a set of UI components, each one providing a view on one or more data sources. The construction of such data views and their visualizations are managed by the *UI Component Manager*, a front-end module that instantiates each UI component based on the data sets built by the mashup engine. The logic of the UI Component Manager is determined by *UI Templates*. UI Templates are cornerstone elements in EFESTO, both for the way the users perceive the mechanisms for building UI components, and for the data integration logic behind the construction of the components data sets. Indeed, on the one hand, UI Templates provide the users with a schematic representation of how data extracted from services will be organized (i.e., aggregated and visualized) within each single UI component [5, 8]. On the other hand, at the Logic Layer UI templates then provide *data integration schemas*, as they determine how the mashup engine has to query the involved data sources and integrate the resulting data. Indeed, by associating selected service attributes to UI template elements, the composer defines a projection of the only attributes of interest. In addition, if the attributes associated to a single UI template element are selected from multiple services, then the structure of the UI template determines a *global integration schema* mapping the attributes of single services into an integrated data set. These actions captured at the interaction level are then translated into the specification, within a UI component descriptor, of service queries and data fusion procedures used by the mashup engine to build the integrated data sets [8].

As represented in Fig. 4, each UI component displays a set of *UI items*, i.e., data elements rendered according to the layout provided by the UI template. UI items are the atomic elements composition actions can be applied to. Starting from a UI item, the users can expand the mashup data set by defining data integration operations (union and join) with data sets of additional services. The selection of a UI item can provide an entry point for the exploration in the LOD. The user can also achieve coordinated visualizations of the UI Components by *synchronizing* the event of selecting a UI item in a component with the activation of operations that can change the status of other components (e.g., to achieve a different data set filtering or a new visualization).

Given a UI component, *transitions* among different UI templates are possible to achieve different data organizations (e.g., from a table highlighting detailed properties of each single data instance to a mind map highlighting the relationship among different instances) and visualizations (e.g., from a list of addresses to a map based representation of the same data). Transitions, however, imply the need of modelling the structure of the data items originally extracted from data sources, to be able to trace and identify the transformations needed when moving the items across different visualizations. For this reason, each service, when registered, is associated with a set of possible *service visualizations*, i.e., the specification of UI templates families (i.e., lists, maps, charts, graphs) that can be properly used to render the service data. The mapping between the service data attributes and specific UI items in charge of attributes rendering is also defined.

The live programming paradigm, which allows the users to see immediately the effect of their actions on the mashup under construction, is achieved by means of *Event Listeners* that are able to catch the events generated by the user actions (e.g., the drag of a service attribute to a field of a UI template) and send them to an *Event Manager*. This module of the Mashup Engine, located in the Logic Layer, is in charge of translating events into the proper invocation of services whose effect is the refresh of the status of the mashup and of its UI components, depending on the captured events.

3.2 Logic Layer

The Logic Layer provides for modules and mechanisms that translate the user composition actions operated at the Interaction Layer into the mashup executing logic. We here describe the different modules supposing that they are deployed separately from the Interaction Layer modules, i.e., on a back-end server. However, **the Logic Layer can be distributed between the client and the server** or, at the other extreme, located only at the **client-side** if the execution context requires a single-user, lightweight deployment. Server-side execution offers the advantage of managing a **long lasting instantiation logic** with the additional possibility of supporting **multi-user mashups**, **collaborative composition** paradigms, and the **distributed execution of interactive workspaces**, as we already discussed in some previous papers [7].

3.2.1 The Mashup Engine

The *Mashup Engine* is invoked by the UI Component Manager each time an event, requiring the retrieval of new data or the invocation of service operations, is generated at the interaction layer. For instance, when the user specifies a search key to filter a component data set, the typed key and the component identifier are passed to the Mashup Engine. The Mashup Engine retrieves from a dedicated repository the

XML-based *UI Component Descriptor*, and inspects it to identify all the services used in the mashup. Figure 5 illustrates an example of UI component descriptor where SongKick is joined with YouTube. Based on this specification, the Mashup Engine retrieves from the Service Descriptor repository all the XML descriptors associated with the services involved in the mashup (SongKick and YouTube in Fig. 5). Each service descriptor is sent to the *Source Dispatcher* that, depending on the specified service type, invokes specific adapters to retrieve the data. In fact, our platform can manage different types of data sources, like RESTful and SOAP services, databases, files (e.g., csv, excel) and Linked Open Data. If a new type of data source needs to be registered in the platform, a new adapter has to be developed. Depending on the nature of the data source, the Source Dispatcher instantiates an adapter available in the *Source Manager* package that implements the logic for querying the specific type of data source. Moreover, if a data source demands for an authentication, the *Authentication Manager* provides for different classes implementing different types of authentication, like *OAUTH 2.0, OpenID* and *Custom Authentications*.

```xml
<?xml version="1.0" encoding="UTF-8"?>
<composition join="true" union="false">
  <base_service name="songkick_by_artist" hyperlink="false">
    <attribute name="Event_name" path="displayName">displayName</attribute>
    <attribute name="Type" path="type">type</attribute>
    <attribute name="Date" path="start.date">start.date</attribute>
    <attribute name="StarTime" path="start.time">start.time</attribute>
    <attribute name="City" path="location.city">location.city</attribute>
    <attribute name="longitude" path="location.lng">location.lng</attribute>
    <attribute name="latitude" path="location.lat">location.lat</attribute>
    <attribute name="Artist" path="performance[0].artist.displayName">performance[0].artist.displayName</attribute>
    <attribute name="SongKick_WebPage" path="uri">uri</attribute>
  </base_service>
  <unions>
  </unions>
  <joins>
    <join type="composition">
      <service name="youtube" />
      <input>Artist</input>
      <extendedAttributes>
        <attribute name="Title" path="snippet.title">snippet.title</attribute>
        <attribute name="Video" path="id.videoId">id.videoId</attribute>
      </extendedAttributes>
    </join>
  </joins>
</composition>
```

Fig. 5. XML *UI Component* descriptor: the SongKick service is joined with YouTube through the Artist attribute

After querying each service as modelled in the *UI Component Descriptor*, the *Result Builder* creates the final data set, codified in JSON, and sends it back to the UI component manager. Figure 6 represents an example of JSON array produced by querying the mashup shown in Fig. 5. Finally, the UI Component Manager builds the UI view to render the JSON data according to the layout of the component UI template.

3.2.2 The Event Manager

Another important module in the Logic Layer is the *Event Manger*. It is in charge of translating any composition action into proper descriptors, and to enact immediately service invocations to achieve the corresponding behaviour in the mashup under construction. When the users operate on a mashup the visual actions are caught by the *Event Listener* at the Interaction Layer and sent to the Event Manger. For example, at the beginning of our reference scenario, Michael creates the SongKick UI component by means of a wizard procedure that guides him to choose the data source (SongKick) and the UI template (Map), and to associate through drag&drop actions the SongKick attributes to the UI template fields. When Michael saves the SongKick mashup, two descriptors are created. The first one is similar to the one reported in Fig. 5 (except for the *<joins>* tag that does not have any children when Songkick is created). When users expand the data source by joining and unifying it with other sources, the *<joins>* and *<unions>* tags are enriched with specific children.

The second XML file then defines the mapping between the data attributes included in the mashup (as described in the first descriptor) and the chosen UI template (whose structure is in turn described in an XML file stored in the Service Visualizations repository).

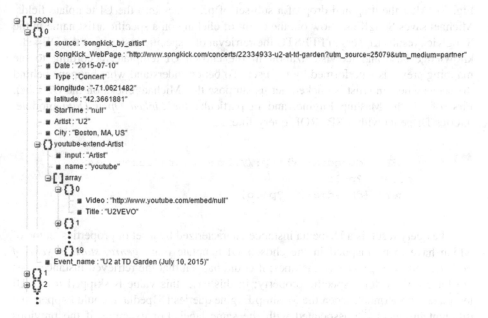

```
⊟ [ ] JSON
  ⊟ { } 0
     ▪ source : "songkick_by_artist"
     ▪ SongKick_WebPage : "http://www.songkick.com/concerts/22334933-u2-at-td-garden?utm_source=25079&utm_medium=partner"
     ▪ Date : "2015-07-10"
     ▪ Type : "Concert"
     ▪ longitude : "-71.0621482"
     ▪ latitude : "42.3661881"
     ▪ StarTime : "null"
     ▪ Artist : "U2"
     ▪ City : "Boston, MA, US"
     ⊟ { } youtube-extend-Artist
        ▪ input : "Artist"
        ▪ name : "youtube"
        ⊟ [ ] array
           ⊟ { } 0
              ▪ Video : "http://www.youtube.com/embed/null"
              ▪ Title : "U2VEVO"
           ⊞ { } 1
             ⋮
           ⊞ { } 19
     ▪ Event_name : "U2 at TD Garden (July 10, 2015)"
  ⊞ { } 1
  ⊞ { } 2
     ⋮
```

Fig. 6. JSON array produced by the Mashup Engine invoked on the *UI Component* descriptor shown in Fig. 5 with the *"U2"* query

3.2.3   The Annotation Engine and the Polymorphic Data Source
During our field studies, we noticed that very often, during the process of exploring information, end users were forced to leave the platform to perform their tasks through traditional search engines. To overcome this limitation and better satisfy the end users' information needs, we introduced a new polymorphic data source built upon the LOD cloud, and in particular exploiting the DBpedia knowledge base.

In order to create the polymorphic data source, a mapping step is required between all the data sources registered in the platform and the DBpedia ontology classes.

The main goal of this mapping is to annotate the attributes of each service by using a DBpedia class that is semantically similar to the attribute. In fact, each time the EFESTO administrator registers a new service through the administration panel, the *Service Registration Manager* (a module of the Web front-end) asks the administrator to type some example queries (at most a dozen) to automatically annotate the service attributes. The service descriptor, together with the provided example queries, is sent to the *Annotation Engine* that automatically generates the service attribute annotations [9], which are then stored in the *Semantic Annotation* repository.

Now let us come back to the Michael scenario and suppose that he wants to join the SongKick Artist attribute with DBpedia. After he decides to use DBpedia as extension data source, the Event Manager triggers the retrieval, by the source manager, of the XML file with the annotations associated with SongKick. The class used to annotate the artist attribute (*MusicalArtist* class) is then extracted from the DBpedia ontology. Afterwards, the wizard procedure shows to Michael all the MusicalArtist properties as attributes that he can choose to build the joined data source (see the highlighted box in Fig. 7). After the drag and drop of a sub-set of properties into the UI template fields, Michael saves SongKick. Now on, the event of clicking on a specific artist name in the SongKick results triggers in EFESTO the retrieval of a specific instance of the DBpedia knowledge base and its visualization in the chosen UI template, according to the mapping previously performed by the user. To better understand what happens behind the scene when an artist is clicked, let us suppose that Michael clicks on the *U2* label. First of all, the Mashup Engine, and in particular the *Linked Open Data* module, queries DBpedia with a SPARQL query like:

```
PREFIX dbpedia: <http://dbpedia.org/resource/>
select ?p ?o
where {dbpedia:U2 ?p ?o}
```

The query result is a DBpedia instance characterized by a set of properties, some of which have to be mapped in the chosen UI template (e.g., *genre, starting year of activity*, and *artist photo*). Sometimes, it could happen that the retrieved instance does not have a value for a specific property; in this case, this value is skipped in the UI template. Furthermore, when the Mashup Engine queries DBpedia, it could happen that different instances are associated with the same label. For example, if the previous query includes the *Ligabue* search key instead of *U2*, five instances are retrieved: Antonio Ligabue, an Italian painter; Giancarlo Ligabue, an Italian palaeontologist; Ilva Ligabue, an Italian operatic soprano; Ligabue, a TV drama; Luciano Ligabue, the Italian singer (our target). To identify the right instance (Luciano Ligabue), the system checks which one is a sub-class of the class used to annotate the artist attribute, namely *MusicalArtist* in the Michael's scenario. This example highlights the dual role of service attribute annotations, which are used (i) during the mapping phase, to show the DBpedia class properties that the users can move into the UI Template fields (Fig. 7) and (ii) during the execution of a SPARQL query, to disambiguate multiple retrieved instances.

3.3 Service and Data Layer

Through the *Service and Data* layer, the EFESTO Web server exposes repositories of XML-based descriptors that enable the invocation of services to extract data.

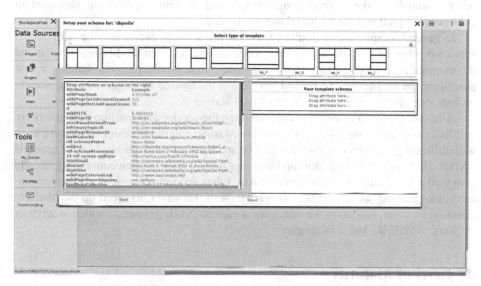

Fig. 7. Mapping step between the DBpedia-based polymorphic data source properties and the list UI template

The *Service Descriptors* provide abstract specifications on how to query each data source registered in the platform and how to read its results. The *Workspace Descriptors* then contain representations of the workspaces created by each user. For each workspace, a descriptor specifies the included UI components and possible UI synchronizations defined among them. The UI Component Descriptors then specify the services included into the components, the user-defined queries to integrate the services data sets (see Fig. 5), and the specification of the component UI template.

The Workspace and UI Component descriptors are associated to the user who creates them, and thus can be accessed depending on the users' access rights. Some "default" workspace descriptors are also available to any user; they provide the specification for pre-packaged workspaces related to specific topics or domains. In fact, users can compose their mashups starting from an empty workspace (like in Michael scenario) or choosing a thematic template filled with some ready-to-use UI Components that are relevant for particular domains/topics.

The *Semantic Annotations* repository stores the files used to describe the DBpedia classes associated to each service attribute. Finally, the *Service Visualizations* descriptors provide the abstract representations (in terms of offered UI elements) of the available UI templates.

The definition of the service descriptors and semantic annotation is a technical task that could be out of reach for non-programmers and, as such, could limit the introduction of new services within the platform by end users.. To alleviate this problem, the definition of descriptors and annotations is facilitated by visual forms that only require inserting some values; then the XML specification is automatically generated by the system. Also, we envisage the adoption of our platform in meta-design scenarios, where other stakeholders (i.e., expert programmers and domain experts) are supposed to configure the platform for its initial use by the end users.

In general, despite the difficulties that end users might encounter, the adoption of service descriptors and adapters enables a decoupling between the Mashup Engine and the external resources so that adding a new data source only requires defining a new descriptor; an adapter is also needed but only if the Source Manager does not already include one able to manage that type of data source.

A further aspect to be noted is that, although the service and mashup descriptors are codified using a custom XML grammar, the Mashup Engine is designed to work even with different grammars designed for service and mashup descriptions, like for example EMML (Enterprise Mashup Markup Language)[3] for which an open community already provided a large amount of descriptors. Any other service ecosystem, where services are homogeneously described, would work as well. However, to speed up the platform development and validation we opted for a custom XML grammar, which is anyway inspired to EMML, but it is simpler.

4 Level of Maturity

The current version of the EFESTO platform is the results of a 4-years research. During this period, we adopted a user-centred approach with the main goal of identifying how a mashup composition paradigm could really help the users themselves. Our research is indeed strongly inspired by and oriented towards End-User Development principles [11]. We therefore conducted several user studies to elicit end-user requirements with respect to the composition of mashups [6] and to validate our design choices and their consequent implementation in the platform [7, 8]. These studies show that EFESTO can be adopted by users without specific expertise in programming with a good level of effectiveness, efficiency, and satisfaction.

These findings are true for several application domains. The EFESTO architecture and the composition paradigm have been indeed designed having in mind customization as a mean to ease the adoption of the platform by different communities of end users, each one featuring specific requirements, background and expertise. In particular, we have investigated meta-design approaches, where different stakeholders (e.g., developers, graphic designers, domain experts) customize different elements of the platform (e.g., UI components, UI templates, visual composition mechanisms) and create artifacts that the end users can exploit profitably [5, 7]. In the end, thanks to this methodological framework, end users can use or customize the platform in different modalities, depending on their expertise and willingness to be engaged in the creation of artifacts: from the visual composition of ready-to-use UI components created by other and more

---

[3] http://mdc.jackbe.com/prestodocs/v3.8/index.html.

expert stakeholders, to the definition of their own components by means of the mashup operations illustrated above in this paper, to the development of new UI templates in casw a specific application domain requires for different types of data visualizations.

We validated our approach to customization in different contexts. One extensive experimentation was conducted in the Cultural Heritage domain, when our platform was customized to support professional tourist guides. The emerging need in this scenario was to enhance the visits lead by the guides in an archeological park with the possibility to create flexibly multi-device mashups to show to the visitors complementary multimedia material retrieved by different (both public and private) online sources [5, 7, 12].

Another customization experience is then related to the adoption of EFESTO in a Technology-Enhanced Learning (TEL) scenario. In this context students learn about a topic presented in class by their teacher, then complement the teacher's lesson by searching information on the Web, and communicate and share the results of their search with the teacher and other students [7]. Nowadays, schools are provided with different computing devices, not only desktop but also tablets and interactive whiteboards. Teachers and students are increasingly using such devices and various software tools in their daily activities.

A further interesting scenario in which we have customized and we are experimenting EFESTO is the living labs of the VINCENTE (A Virtual collective INtelligenCe ENvironment to develop sustainable Technology Entrepreneurship ecosystems) research project. The aim of the project is to design, implement and test methodological and technological platforms that use services to create ecosystems for sustainable entrepreneurship, which optimize the use of resources, enhance the knowledge, respect the environment and ethical values and ensure the social inclusion. Our current work is devoted to the customization of EFESTO to the specific requirements related to the establishment of collaborative entrepreneurial ecosystems.

5 Related Work

The problem of facilitating the access to Web services and APIs through mashup tools has been attracting the attention of several researchers, who in the last years focused on different issues. From an HCI perspective, empowering a larger class of users to create their own applications requires intuitive abstraction mechanisms, easy development tools and a high level of assistance. Therefore, some research projects have been dealing with the problem of enabling the creation of effective presentations on top of Web services and APIs, to provide a direct channel between the user and the service (e.g. [13]). They focused on the notion of Web Service Graphical User Interfaces (WSGUIs) [14], i.e., on a set of mechanisms to enrich the Web service specifications with annotations that could make the definition of visual interfaces easy.

The previous approaches do not allow the composition of multiple services in an integrated application. In some cases, building a complete Web application equipped with a user interface requires the adoption of additional tools or technologies. Recently, different approaches have been proposed to blend design and execution environments while exploiting intuitive mechanisms to define mashups. For example, NaturalMash allows one to express in natural language what service(s) the users want to use and how to synchronize them [15]. To ensure the accuracy of the expressed user queries, NaturalMash narrows the user in a controlled natural language (a subset of a natural language with a limited vocabulary and grammar). If on the one hand the users have only to type assisted queries to mashup services, on the other hand this paradigm inherits all the natural language processing problems and limitations.

A completely different approach is described in [16] where the authors propose a new perspective on the problem of data integration on the Web, the Surface Web. The idea is to consider Web pages UI elements as interactive artefacts that enable the access to a set of operations that can be performed on the artefacts. For example, a user can integrate into his personal Web page a list of videos gathered from YouTube and can also append a list of Vimeo videos. This data integration can also be improved by means of filtering and ordering mechanisms. These operations can be performed, for example, by pointing and clicking elements (YouTube and Vimeo video lists), dragging and dropping them into a target page (e.g. personal Web page), choosing options (filtering and ordering). As highlighted by the authors, despite this approach is very promising, some limitations still affect this solution, for example, low performance (UIs need to be instantiated locally), the missing support for more advanced use cases beyond data integration and heterogeneity of structured data in the Web.

As we have illustrated in this paper, in our approach the integration of different services is guided by UI templates, which implicitly provide an integration schema and therefore do not require the users to specify the mapping of service attributes with a global integration schema. Mechanisms similar to UI templates are adopted also in other approaches for the composition of service-based interactive applications, but from a different perspective. For example, in the mashup composition approach presented in [13], a so-called service front end is a form-based UI module that gives a representation of the technical interface of a Web service and provides the users with the list of parameters expected by the service. The user can specify values for such parameters, depending on the needed content. The resulting application is thus able at runtime to query the service and visualize the results in a tabular template. Our UI templates also offer support to query services, but through a paradigm that seamlessly allows the user to define integrated views over different services. Our UI templates then introduce additional abstractions, which go beyond pure service querying as they guide the users in a data integration process resulting into integrated visualizations.

Other recent approaches to perform mashup focus on distributed and/or multi-screen mashups. Among them, the SmartComposition approach [17] enables the end users to easily create multi-screen mashups in terms of different widgets distributed and synchronized on different devices like PC, smartphone, smart TV. For example, a teacher can create a distributed mashup to present his lesson with a laptop connected to a projector and deliver additional information to participants' mobile devices. Even though the development of distributed, multi-device mashups is not discussed in this paper, we also worked on extending EFESTO to allow multiple users to collaboratively construct and execute mashups across different devices. In fact, the workspaces created in EFESTO can be shared among different users so that they can synchronously collaborate in creating and manipulating new information. The available mechanisms for sharing and collaboration are inspired to the ones of Google Drive. Moreover, chat, annotations and offline messages also support asynchronous collaboration. We validated the devised extensions, and especially their usefulness for the end users, in a user study in the Technology Enhanced Learned domain [7]. The users were satisfied of the devised collaborative mechanisms and found them very useful. However, they expressed the need to further "manipulate" the collaboratively-created workspaces through functions that could allow them to accomplish collaboratively some situational tasks. It was this study that suggested us to move towards the notion of *actionable mashups* [10], i.e., interactive workspaces where users could also invoke tools to manipulate the integrated data across several dimensions. Such new features permit the transition of information between different *task containers*, i.e., dedicated, contextual task environments that, according to the recently proposed notion of Transformative User Experience [18], can support users in accomplishing in an elastic way their tasks. We believe this feature, scarcely explored in literature and not investigated in other mashup platforms, provides for a very innovative direction that could give value to mashups as tools to let users to make sense of data for accomplishing their tasks.

6   ICWE 2015 Rapid Mashup Challenge

During the Rapid Mashup Challenge, we illustrated the EFESTO characteristics described above by means of a demo that followed the same flow of actions as the reference scenario described in Sect. 2. The mashup built on the fly included the services SongKick, YouTube, Vimeo, Google Maps and Google Images, and allowed us to demonstrate: (1) how to define a union of the YouTube and Vimeo data sets; (2) how to join the SongKick Artist attribute (visualized in a Map UI Template) with YouTube; (3) how to shift from a map UI template to a list UI Template for the SongKick UI Component; and (4) how to synchronize at the UI level the new data set with Google Maps (showing the location of selected music events) and Google Images (showing images of the cities where the events take place). During the demo, we also showed how to extend the integrated information retrieved by this core set of services by navigating in the LOD.

Getting prepared for the challenge actually did not require additional efforts as the services mashed up during the demo were already registered in the platform. We only made sure that their descriptors and the adapters for invoking them were running correctly. A problem compromising the correct behaviour of the platform, which is anyway common to many mashup platforms, could be the change of APIs for the registered services, which could compromise their invocation by the platform.

During the demo everything worked perfectly; we wished we had more time to demonstrate some features that we recently introduced in EFESTO that, as described in the previous section, relate to the notion of actionable mashups. The readers interested in these extensions can find more details in [10], and watch the video available at: https://youtu.be/bBG5O266y4g (min 4:00–6:10).

7 Conclusions

In several application domains there is an increasing demand by end users to access, integrate, and use flexibly multiple resources available online. The EFESTO platform tries to respond to this need by letting users easily integrate, by means of an End-User Development paradigm, heterogeneous information that otherwise would be totally unrelated. This approach is very useful in all those situations where, due to varying information needs exposed by the end users, a pre-packaged application could not work properly. The modus operandi promoted by the EFESTO approach also facilitates the construction of new knowledge and its continuous enrichment in contexts where the establishment of communities implies the collaborative creation of knowledge.

This paper described how, in addition to what offered by other platforms, EFESTO also enables a seamless transition of the retrieved data across different organizations, visualizations and functionality. We believe this is a characterizing feature that can pave the way to a new conception of mashups as effective tools for supporting users' tasks and we are devoting several efforts to formalizing the new interaction model for characterizing the possible transitions across different data organizations. The potential of the interaction paradigm was also recognized at the Mashup Challenge. The comments of the jury and of the participants were very positive; and in the end we won the challenge! We also received very encouraging feedback on the idea of including LOD data sources. Our current work is devoted to consolidating LOD navigation and extending the current mechanisms by means of recommendations.

Acknowledgment. This work is partially supported by the Italian Ministry of University and Research (MIUR) under grants PON02_00563_3470993 "VINCENTE", PON04a2_B "EDOC@WORK3.0", and PON03PE_00136_1 "DSE" and by the Italian Ministry of Economic Development (MISE) under grant PON Industria 2015 MI01_00294 "LOGIN". We are also immensely grateful to Prof. Maria Francesca Costabile for her valuable and constant support.

References

1. Daniel, F., Matera, M.: Mashups: Concepts. Models and Architectures. Springer, Berlin (2014)
2. White, R.W., Roth, R.A.: Exploratory search: beyond the query-response paradigm. Synth. Lect. Inf. Concepts Retrieval Serv. 1(1), 1–98 (2009)
3. Namoun, A., Nestler, T., De Angeli, A.: Conceptual and usability issues in the composable web of software services. In: Daniel, F., Facca, F.M. (eds.) ICWE 2010. LNCS, vol. 6385, pp. 396–407. Springer, Heidelberg (2010)
4. Casati, F.: How end-user development will save composition technologies from their continuing failures. In: Costabile, M.F., Dittrich, Y., Fischer, G., Piccinno, A. (eds.) IS-EUD 2011. LNCS, vol. 6654, pp. 4–6. Springer, Heidelberg (2011)
5. Ardito, C., Costabile, M.F., Desolda, G., Lanzilotti, R., Matera, M., Piccinno, A., Picozzi, M.: User-driven visual composition of service-based interactive spaces. J. Vis. Lang. Comput. 25(4), 278–296 (2014)

6. Ardito, C., Costabile, M.F., Desolda, G., Lanzilotti, R., Matera, M., Picozzi, M.: Visual composition of data sources by end-users. In: Proceedings of International Working Conference on Advanced Visual Interfaces (AVI), pp. 257–260. Como, Italy, 28–30 May 2014
7. Ardito, C., Bottoni, P., Costabile, M.F., Desolda, G., Matera, M., Picozzi, M.: Creation and use of service-based distributed interactive workspaces. J. Vis. Lang. Comput. 25(6), 717–726 (2014)
8. Cappiello, C., Matera, M., Picozzi, M.: A Ui-centric approach for the end-user development of multidevice mashups. ACM Trans. Web 9(3), 1–40 (2015)
9. Desolda, G.: Enhancing workspace composition by exploiting linked open data as a polymorphic data source. In: Damiani, E., Howlett, R.J., Jain, L.C., Gallo, L., De Pietro, G. (eds.) Intelligent Interactive Multimedia Systems and Services, vol. 40, pp. 97–108. Springer International Publishing (2015)
10. Ardito, C., Costabile, M.F., Desolda, G., Latzina, M., Matera, M.: Making mashups actionable through elastic design principles. In: Díaz, P., Pipek, V., Ardito, C., Jensen, C., Aedo, I., Boden, A. (eds.) IS-EUD 2015. LNCS, vol. 9083, pp. 236–241. Springer, Heidelberg (2015)
11. Costabile, M.F., Fogli, D., Mussio, P., Piccinno, A.: Visual interactive systems for end-user development: a model-based design methodology. IEEE Trans. Syst. Man Cybern. Part A Syst. Hum. 37(6), 1029–1046 (2007)
12. Ardito, C., Costabile, M.F., Desolda, G., Matera, M., Piccinno, A., Picozzi, M.: Composition of situational interactive spaces by end users: a case for cultural heritage. In: Proceedings of Nordic Conference on Human-Computer Interaction (NordiCHI), pp. 79–88, Copenhagen, Denmark, 15–18 October 2012
13. Krummenacher, R., Norton, B., Simperl, E., Pedrinaci, C.: Soa4all: enabling web-scale service economies. In: Proceedings of International Conference on Semantic Computing (ICSC), pp. 535–542, Berkeley, CA, USA, 14–16 September 2009
14. Wajid, U., Namoun, A., Mehandjiev, N.: Alternative representations for end user composition of service-based systems. In: Costabile, M.F., Dittrich, Y., Fischer, G., Piccinno, A. (eds.) IS-EUD 2011. LNCS, vol. 6654, pp. 53–66. Springer, Heidelberg (2011)
15. Aghaee, S., Pautasso, C.: End-user development of mashups with naturalmash. J. Vis. Lang. Comput. 25(4), 414–432 (2014)
16. Daniel, F.: Live, personal data integration through UI-oriented computing. In: Cimiano, P., Frasincar, F., Houben, G.-J., Schwabe, D. (eds.) ICWE 2015. LNCS, vol. 9114, pp. 479–497. Springer, Heidelberg (2015)
17. Krug, M., Wiedemann, F., Gaedke, M.: Smartcomposition: a component-based approach for creating multi-screen mashups. In: Casteleyn, S., Rossi, G., Winckler, M. (eds.) ICWE 2014. LNCS, vol. 8541, pp. 236–253. Springer, Heidelberg (2014)
18. Latzina, M., Beringer, J.: Transformative User Experience: Beyond Packaged Design. Interactions 19(2), 30–33 (2012)

Web Mashups with WebMakeup

Oscar Díaz[1]([⊠]), Iñigo Aldalur[1], Cristóbal Arellano[1], Haritz Medina[1],
and Sergio Firmenich[2,3]

[1] University of the Basque Country (UPV/EHU), San Sebastián, Spain
{oscar.diaz,inigo.aldalur,cristobal.arellano}@ehu.es
[2] Universidad Nacional de la Patagonia San Juan Bosco,
Comodoro Rivadavia, Argentina
[3] CONICET, Buenos Aires, Argentina
sergio.firmenich@lifia.info.unlp.edu.ar

Abstract. Modding refers to the act of modifying hardware, software, or
virtually anything else, to perform a function not originally conceived or
intended by the designer. The rationales for modding should be sought
in the aspiration of users to contextualize to their own situation the
artefact at hand. Websites are not exception. *WebMakeup* targets mod
scenarios where web pages are turned into canvases users can tune to
account for their situational, idiosyncratic, and potentially, short-lived
needs. By clicking, users turn DOM nodes into widgets. Widgets can next
be rearranged, deleted, updated or stored for later reuse in other pages. In
addition, widgets can be involved in "blink" patterns where interactions
with a widget might affect the related widgets. This empowers users to
tune not only *what* but also *when* content is to show up in an AJAX-like
way. *WebMakeup* is publicly available as a Chrome extension.

1 Context and Goals

A mashup has been defined as "a composite application developed starting from
reusable data, application logic, and/or user interfaces typically, but not mandatorily, sourced from the Web" [2]. It has been observed that mashups tend to
be limited in their scope, addressing what is being referred to as *the long tail*
of the software market whose limited demands and/or benefits make mashups
fall outside mainstream applications [2]. This observation rises the question of
who develops mashups, i.e., the profile of those addressing *the long tail*. Hence,
it is relevant to start by first characterizing this audience. Differences between
mashup tools frequently rest on the different user profiles being targeted. In
other words, tool success very much depends on the accuracy to which these
profiles are pinpointed.

Our mashup scenario is characterized as being situational, idiosyncratic and,
potentially, short-lived. These aspects challenge traditional software development, and shift the focus from professional programmers to hobby programmers
or even, laymen. This changes the rules of the game. Available time, available
skills or motivation greatly differ depending on the target developers. For professional programmers, development takes place in a working setting where time

© Springer International Publishing Switzerland 2016
F. Daniel and C. Pautasso (Eds.): RMC 2015, CCIS 591, pp. 82–97, 2016.
DOI: 10.1007/978-3-319-28727-0_6

and skills are assumed, and motivation is turned into duty. This setting changes when development is handed over to laymen. It might well be part of work or not. Some support might be available but most of the time, development is conducted on layman's own account. Basically, we characterize our target audience (i.e. the mashup developer) along three features:

1. available expertise: no programming experience. Our target audience should not need to known HTML, APIs, JavaScript or other programming environment in which mashup are realized.
2. available time: 30'. The expectation is for the mashup to be developed in around 30'
3. sparking motivation: improving the Web Experience.

Broadly, our approach can be characterized as follows. First, and unlike traditional mashup approaches, we do not aim at creating a brand new application (the mashup) but customizing an exising one. Second, we do not consider any kind of data source but HTML pages. The term "modding" is used to refer to the possibility of users to tune HTML content and interactions to fit their own patterns. The ultimate goal is improving the User Experience (UX). This is achieved through *modding* mashups (here after referred to as "mods"). This vision accounts for a post-production (i.e. once the modded website is in operation), user-driven Web customization. This paper describes *WebMakeup*, a Chrome plug-in for mod development. Specifically, we focus on the mashup side of *WebMakeup*, i.e. how *WebMakeup* allows for copying HTML fragment from the Web to be later pasted into the modded website. A more complete account of *WebMakeup's* functionality can be found at [4]. This paper focuses on the case study at the Mashup Contest held at the International Conference on Web Engineering (ICWE) in 2015.

2   A Mod Scenario

Consider a layman browsing *The New York Times* website (NYT). What can make him mod this website? Better said, how strong should this mod desire be for the user getting down to work and develop a mod? Although motivations vary, a common source of discomfort is when other websites need to be visited. This might involve opening new tabs, and moving back and forth between different tabs. This makes the user loose focus and break the reading flow. Consider three scenarios when reading the NYT (see Fig. 1):

1. the user is a frequent traveller between Amsterdam Central Station and Rotterdam Central Station. Periodically, the user checks when the next train leaves. NYT is often read while waiting at the train station. Checking next train, involves googling in a new tab,
2. the user is a broker. He needs to keep an eye on share prices even when reading the newspaper,
3. the user likes to check how headlines are covered by media other than the NYT (e.g. NBC news).

4. the user is interested in two sections of the NYT: Science and Sports. He doesn't always check them fully but like to have a glance to the headlines in these sections

These scenarios involve a tab shifting from the NYT website to other websites. Despite its simplicity, the few clicks involve might well break the reading flow. This is not a main discomfort except if conducted in a regular basis. If you are a frequent train traveler, working as a broker, curious about NBC news coverage, or interested in Science and Sports, tab shifting might be a main discomfort in your UX when accessing the NYT website. Modding might help by moving scattered Web content to the website when the main task is conducted, in this case the NYT website. Next section addresses how this NYT scenario can be tackled by *WebMakeup*.

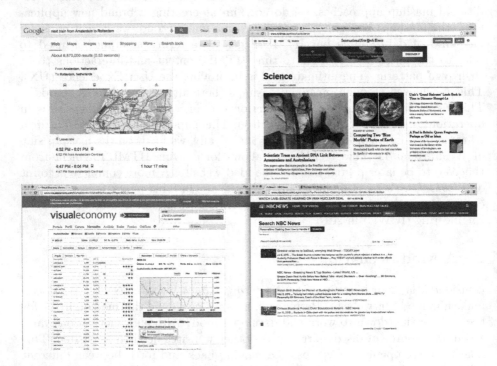

Fig. 1. Websites accessed while reading the NYT (in clockwise order): Google search, Science section of the NYT, Visual Economy, and search facility at the NBC website.

3   A Session with *WebMakeup*

WebMakeup is both an editor and an engine for Web modding. As an editor, it offers a GUI for obtaining mods. As an engine, it interprets mods, and modifies the target page accordingly. *WebMakeup* is available at the *Chrome Web Store*: https://chrome.google.com/webstore/detail/alnhegodephpjnaghlcemlnpdknhbhjj. Usability studies were conducted and reported at [4]. This section describes the creation of a mod for supporting the NYT scenario.

The process starts by the user focusing on the website causing the discomfort. If discomfort is due to visual clutter, then he can start by removing some content. If discomfort is due to disperse content, then he can start by singling out this content, and somehow making it appear at the host website. Finally, he should decide whether all content should be readily available or rather, become visible provided some user interaction occurs. More specifically, this notion of content *that is singled out to be operated upon* is captured in terms of a "widget". For our purposes, a widget is basically an HTML fragment that is being singling out and equipped with some operations and additional meta-properties. Therefore, modding is achieved in terms of widgets, specifically, through four main interventions: widget creation, widget mining, widget handling and widget animation. Next subsections present each intervention with the help of the running example.

3.1 Widget Creation

WebMakeup is a plugin for *Google Chrome*. Its installation is reflected by the *WebMakeup* button at the right of the address bar. On clicking this button, a scrollable menu pops up (see Fig. 2). Clicking on *"New"* causes the following effects:

Fig. 2. The *WebMakeup* scrollable menu.

1. the current page is turned into an editor canvas where the pointer is turned into a camera,
2. a grid-like structure is interspersed on top of the current DOM tree, and
3. two tabs pops up: the *piggyBank* tab and the *patterns* tab.

By mousing over the page, the underlying DOM nodes are highlighted. By clicking, the user singles this node out as a meaningful HTML fragment, i.e. a widget. A limitation is the handling of "hidden nodes", i.e. DOM nodes that do not have a graphical counterpart and hence, they cannot be pinpointed through the cursor. For instance, a table row ($<tr>$) is graphically hidden if its graphical space is totally taken by its content. If the row does not explicitly have some graphical counterpart (e.g. a border), then all the space is occupied by the row's content so that the cursor will always select the row's content rather than the row element itself. To overcome this problem, we resort to the keyboard. Keys "*w*", "*s*", "*a*" and "*d*" help to move up, down, left and right along the DOM tree, respectively, w.r.t to the node being pinpointed by the cursor.

No matter the mechanism (i.e. cursor vs. keyword), the selected node is surrounded by a decorator. In other words, the HTML fragment is turned into a widget, and hence, amenable to be manipulated. Figure 3 depicts the DOM nodes from the NYT website once three DOM nodes are turned into widgets, namely, *linkBar*, *headline*, and *rightColumn*. Broadly, widgets are "those page chunks" to be operated upon in order to be deleted, re-allocated or changed in some of its content. But before moving to widget handling, it is important to note that widgets are not limited to those of the modded page (e.g. the NYT page) but they can be obtained from any place in the Web sphere. This moves us to widget mining.

Fig. 3. DOM nodes are turned into widgets. A decorator permits to operate upon the widget: remove, visibility-state modification and un-widgetization (i.e. turning back to a mere DOM node).

3.2 Widget Mining

For our purposes, Web mashuping involves putting together otherwise scattered Web content. The basic aim: avoiding tab switching and, in some case, copy & paste operations between websites. In the NYT example, we aim at offering train information, stock exchange data or headlines for other newspapers, all without leaving the NYT page. In this example, Google (for the train information), Visual Economy (for the share prices) or NBC (for the headlines) act as the information providers. This information is supported in terms of HTML pages in their respective websites. Therefore, the process goes along a similar pattern as the one described in the previous section, i.e. HTML fragments are turned into widgets. Nevertheless, some subtle differences exist.

Widgets can be mined any time while browsing, not just when creating the mod. To this end, the right-click contextual menu is extended with the *mineIT* item (see Fig. 4). When you come across with a content of interest, select it, and a grid-like structure will be interspersed on top of the current page. Due to mouse hovering, the DOM node under the current cursor location is highlighted. Once the desired node is highlighted, click *mineIT* to be prompted to name the just-created widget. So, mined widgets are kept in the *PiggyBank*, a clipboard-like facility that is later reachable through the *PiggyBank* tab (see later).

Fig. 4. Widget mining from http://www.nbcnews.com/: right click, select *MineIT*, highlight the desired node, and press enter. A popup will request the widget name (e.g. *NBC*). From them on, the widget is kept in the *PiggyBank*.

Worth noting, a mined widget might stand not just for a single node but a set of nodes can be agglutinated upon the same widget as long as all come from the very same page. Just provide the same widget name, and the highlighted node will be merged with the existing widget's structure. The NBC widget is a case in point (see Fig. 4). It aggregates the search bar and the node standing for the first answer. When inlayed, this widget will allow to obtain the first answer without leaving the NYT page.

Besides *NBC*, the running example extracts four widgets (see Fig. 5): namely, *sportHL* from http://www.nytimes.com/pages/sports/international/index.html, *scienceHL* from http://www.nytimes.com/section/science, *stockMarket* from http://www.visualeconomy.com/, and *trainData* from googling "next train from Amsterdam to Rotterdam Central Station". These widgets will be available in the *PiggyBank* clipboard.

From a users perspective, all widgets are obtained in the same way, i.e. through the contextual menu. However, their internal representation might greatly differ based on the underlaying HTML code. Though the technical details are outside the scope of this work [4], readers can gain some insights by looking at the previous examples:

- *sportHL* and *scienceHL*, capture static and always-visible content,
- *trainData* holds also static content but some parts are initially hidden (e.g. trip details) and become visible after some user interaction,
- *stockMarket* holds dynamic data. Share prices are continuously being updated, i.e. frequent server requests are needed to keep the content in sync.

These examples serve to get an insight into the complexities of widgetization. It is rarely the case that just cloning the DOM node will do. More often, CSS and associated JS scripts should also be considered.

3.3 Widget Handling

Previous subsections illustrate how widget can be obtained from the modded page itself or mined from somewhere else. Mined widgets are kept in the *PiggyBank* (available through the namesake tab), and moved to the canvas (i.e. the current page) through drag and drop. Widget placement is automatically handled by the engine through some built-in heuristics. Once on the canvas, all widgets behave the same, i.e.

1. widgets can be deleted or moved around by interacting through the widget decorator,
2. widgets have an initial state, either visible or collapsed, reflected in the decorator through the opened-eye icon or closed-eye icon, respectively (see Fig. 3). At runtime, this state can be changed through user interactions (see Subsect. 3.4) so that widgets move from visible to collapsed, or vice versa,
3. widgets can be parameterized. Parameters are automatically derived based on the underlying HTML fragment. This includes labels, entry form parameters or the refresh polling frequency (for mined widgets). Double click upon the widget to see its parameters.

Fig. 5. Mining widgets for the sample scenario (in clockwise order): *sportHL*, *scienceHL*, *stockMarket* and *trainData*. The widget's node counterpart is highlighted.

Figure 6 shows the parameters after double clicking the *linkBar* widget. Basically, labels and hrefs are made available so that the user can now change any of them. In this case, we change the first link from pointing to the World News to the ICWE program. Parameter assignment can be by value or by reference. By value refers to the user manually providing the value as in the previous example. By reference involves the system automatically retrieving the value by applying an XPath upon the modded page at runtime. XPaths are derived from user interaction upon the host page at parameterization time. Uses do not need to know XPath. The NBC widget is a case in point. This widget's parameters include the searching text. If you type a value, the widget will always look for this value. By contrast, a reference to some content of the NYT page can be set. While the parameter list is visible, go to the canvas, copy the right hand-side headline, and next, paste it as the value of the searching parameter. Internally the engine associates this parameter to the headline's XPath expression. At runtime, the engine enacts the XPath expression and assigns the result to the NBC's searching parameter "Personalities Clashing Over How to Handle Greek Bailout". In this way, the NBC widget will search for the current headline and not for the headline at the time the mod was created.

Fig. 6. Changing *linkBar's* parameters. First hyperlink's label is changed from *World* to *ICWE Program* while its URL now points to the ICWE website.

3.4 Widget Animation

Modding happens in an existing page which will probably have most of its space taken. Indeed, our running example handles seven widgets, namely:

- from the modded page: *linkBar*, *headline*, *rightColumn*
- from the websphere: *trainData*, *stockMarket*, *NBC*, *SportHL*, *ScienceHL*

Displaying all these widgets simultaneously will lead to an even more cluttered NYT page, impacting the UX. Hence, it is common to turn some nodes into widgets with the only purpose of deleting them, and making room for new content. This is the case of *rightColumn*. This widget is removed to leave room for *stockMarket*. But, this might not be enough. We should also consider which widgets should be readily visible (i.e. at loading time), and which should be visible on demand, i.e. subject to a previous user interaction upon another widget. The latter is referred to as widget animation.

Fig. 7. Setting blinks between widgets. Widget below will be visible after clicking on the widget above.

Widgets can be in two states: visible or collapsed. At design time, users decide the initial state. At runtime, this state can be changed through "blinks". *Blink* relationships can be set between widgets so that interactions upon a widget can impact another widget's state. *Blinks* are graphically represented through pipes. Widget decorators have in their right-hand side a yellow circle. This circle denotes a pipe start. Click and drag from this point to expand till reaching another widget. This sets a *blink* from the triggering widget (the pipe's start) to the triggered widget (the pipe's end). An entry field on top of the pipe serves to indicate the blink's event. The default triggering event is *click*, though users can select other DOM events. Figure 7 depicts such a pipe from *headline* to *NBC*. *NBC'* initial state is collapsed. This blink instructs that clicking *headline* will change NBC state. Let's see the rest of the animation (see Fig. 7):

Specifically, buttons can be introduced to make widgets available on demand (i.e. through button interaction).

Let's see a possible animation strategy for our sample case (see Fig. 7):

– *headline* and *stockMarket* are always visible (i.e. they are never involved as triggered widgets in a *blink*),
– *NBC* is initially collapsed. It becomes visible when clicking on *headline*,
– *trainData* is initially collapsed. We introduce the *nextTrain* button to make it available on demand. To this end, *PiggyBank* always holds three handy widgets (i.e. *link*, *image* and *button*) which can be cloned and parameterized as any other widget,
– *sportHL* is initially visible but collapsed when clicking on the *whatElse* button,
– *scienceHL* is initially collapsed but becomes visible when clicking on the *whatElse* button.

The later introduces a disjunction-blink pattern whereby two widgets are shown in alternation on clicking upon a common widget. By letting users play with the tool, we noticed other recurrent composition of blinks:

– **click2erase.** This pattern involves only one widget. It accounts for a single blink. For instance, consider *"stockMarket blinks stockMarket on clicking"*. *stockMarket* will be available till the user click on it. On clicking, *stockMarket* is gone for the current session.
– **click2alternate.** This pattern involves two widgets which are shown alternatively. It accounts for two blinks: *"scienceHL blinks sportHL.state=visible on clicking"* & *"sportHL blinks scienceHL.state=collapse on clicking"*. Initially only *sportHL* is visible. Click on it, and *sportHL* is substituted by *scienceHL*. Click again, and *sportHL* shows up again.
– **conjunction.** These patterns involve three widgets or more: the triggering widgets, and two triggered widgets that are shown simultaneously. It accounts for two blinks: *"whatElse blinks sportHL on clicking"* & *"whatElse blinks scienceHL on clicking"*. On clicking, both *sportHL* and *scienceHL* pops up.
– **disjunction.** These patterns involve three widgets: the triggering widgets, and two triggered widgets that are shown in alternation. It accounts for two blinks: *"whatElse blinks sportHL.state=visible on clicking"* & *"whatElse*

blinks scienceHL.state=collapse on clicking". Clicking successively on *whatElse* shows *sportHL* and *scienceHL* in alternation.

- **incremental.** This pattern involves "n" widgets which are gradually presented as the user clicks. It accounts for "n-1" blinks. The first blink involves the triggering widget (e.g. *"headline blinks sportHL on clicking"*) while subsequent blinks subordinate the rendering of a widget to click in its widget predecessor (e.g. *"sportHL blinks scienceHL on clicking"*). Therefore, widget order matters.
- **domino.** It leverages the previous pattern so that clicking on the last widget collapses all its predecessors except the triggering widget (i.e. *"headline"*).

These patterns are available through the namesake tab. Pattern definition is achieved using a similar approach to PowerPoint's SmartArts (see Fig. 8). Keeping the *ALT* key pressed down, select the involved widgets. As widgets are being selected, the widget region is shadowed, highlighting the order of the widget at hand. Once all the participating widgets are picked out, and keeping the *ALT* key pressed down, choose the desired behavior in the *pattern* tab. *WebMakeup* will automatically generate the blinks that jointly account for the pattern at hand.

4   The Mod Lifecycle

Though previous subsections present the different operations in sequence, the user is free to intermingle those operations as they come to mind. Indeed, we envisage mod development to be characterized as being in "perpetual beta" in the sense of the mod being able to be easily modified at any time. Ease deployment of partial mods allows users to get a glimpse of the development so far. To this end, the *WebMakeup* menu offers the *"Deploy"* option (see Fig. 2). On clicking, the page is reload but with the mod enacted. Now, the user can get a real feeling on the result so far. For instance, Fig. 9 depicts the NYT website with the sample mod. By interacting with the different widget regions, the user can check out the mod's animation. Previous figure depicts the outcome after clicking *nextTrain* and *headline*. Finally, important and export facilities are available for mod sharing through the namesake options in the *WebMakeup* menu. Export generates a *.mkp* file. This file can then be imported, or even easier, dragged and dropped into the browser for the consumer to enjoy the mod.

5   Level of Maturity and Discussion

WebMakeup is available at the *Chrome Web Store*: https://chrome.google.com/webstore/detail/alnhegodephpjnaghlcemlnpdknhbhjj. It is then available for public download. The case study described in this paper was conducted with this plug-in. More complex cases still present main challenges. Mining widgets from content resulting from AJAX interactions is still difficult. Implementation details can be found at [4]. Technically, WebMakeup exhibit some limitations that were highlighted during the Mashup contest:

Fig. 8. Setting patterns. Keeping the *ALT* key pressed down, select first the widgets, and next, the *blink* pattern.

- upgrades on the NYT website can break the mod apart. Since widget placement and data binding are based on the page structure, changes to this structure can make the mod stop working. True. Notice however that re-building the mod from scratch will take around 30', and that after all, the layout of the NYT website does not change so often. However, the risk is there.
- mod reuse might be limited to users exhibiting the same browser settings. By browser settings, we refer to those client-side aspects that might impact the page structure. First, extensions. Mods might not be the only extensions deployed at the user's browser installation. Thousands of extensions are available at browsers' Web stores that might co-exist and interact with mods. A common case is that of ad blockers. These popular extensions prevent adverts from showing up. In so doing, they change the page structure, and hence, they might impact the mod outcome.

Fig. 9. The mod at work. Screenshot once *nextTrain* and *headline* have been clicked.

- incremental development of mods might be penalized by rich, heavy Web pages. The point is that mod enactment takes place once the page is fully downloaded. That is, widgets start showing up once all the server content is being loaded. No way to click *nextTrain* till all the content is available. During the contest, this was a cause of distress since it took several seconds for the NYT page to be fully loaded, hence hindering the quick feedback that *WebMakeup* aims at.
- installability (i.e., the quality of requiring minimum installation burden) is regarded as a main advantage of *WebMakeup*. Being an extension itself, *WebMakeup* can be easily downloaded from *Chrome Web Store*: https://chrome.google.com/webstore/detail/alnhegodephpjnaghlcem lnpdknhbhjj. This makes the *WebMakeup* icon to show up in the browser bar. This is all needed to start modding your favorite websites.

Table 1. Characterizing *WebMakeup* as a mashup tool.

Mashup feature checklist		Mashup tool feature checklist	
Mashup type	UI mashup	**Targeted end-user**	Non programmers
Component types	UI components	**Automation degree**	Semi-automation
Runtime location	Client-side only	**Liveness level**	Level 3[a]
Integration logic	UI-based integration	**Interaction technique**	WYSIWYG
Instantiation lifecycle	Short-living	**Online user community**	Private but sharable

[a]Automatic Compilation and Deployment, requires Re-initialization.

6   Related Work

The first question is whether modding should be considered a mashup technique. The answer is unclear. It might be so in spirit but not in architecture. That is, mods aim at improving the UX, and one way to achieve this is through mashuping, here understood as side-by-side integration of Web content. However, from an architectural perspective, mods are not self-contained Web applications but browser extensions (a.k.a. plugs-in) to be frequently achieved at the back of the website and by users who might not have server access. From this perspective, modding falls within the area of Web Augmentation [3]. Table 1 sets *WebMakeup* within the feature checklist put forward by the Contest organizers:

- mashup components (i.e. the artefact to be reused and that is accessible either locally or remotely) are limited to HTML fragments which are extracted from websites and included in the modded website.
- mashup logic (i.e. the internal logic of operation of a mashup) includes aspects such as widget location within the modded page, data flow between the modded page and the hosted widgets, or widget animation.

Specifically, *WebMakeup* pivots around the notion of "widget". There already exist W3C standards for UI Reuse like Widgets [10] and Web Components [11]. W3C Widgets are "full-fledged client-side applications that are authored using Web standards such as HTML and packaged for distribution". Web Components allow to "Web application authors to define widgets with a level of visual richness and interactivity not possible with CSS alone, and ease of composition and reuse". Reusing such components is possible in our context. However, we decided not to integrate them due to its immaturity and the low number of such components that already exist on the Web.

Another possibility for widget creation is to create them based on a fragment selected by the user. This process comprises two steps: the selection of the area to be widgetized and the extraction of such area. For the selection step, it would be useful any guidance. As introduced earlier, a widget is meaningful piece of information support as a DOM element. It is trivial to allow users the selection of any DOM element. However this is not the same for filter this selection to such elements that are meaningful as a unit. In the accessibility area, there are some works that face the problem of page segmentation. This page segmentation is used to slice a webpage in meaningful units that are later consumed by impaired users [8,9]. These algorithms can be used in our context to guide to end-users while selecting a DOM element. For mirroring the fragment as closely as possible, it would be needed to extract the content, style and functionality of the original webpage. This is far from trivial. Whereas there are multiple libraries to extract content and style automatically [5,6], as far as we know, there is no automatic mechanism to extract the functionality. There are some works that relates user interactions with the JavaScript code that handles them [1,7], in order to help programmers during the maintenance tasks. Departing from such point, it could be possible to extract such code and execute in the augmented web in an automatic way. However, again, this is far from trivial. A possible way could be the programmatic generation of all possible interactions, the extraction and dependency resolution of the executed code and its injection in the augmented page.

Acknowledgments. This work is co-supported by the Spanish Ministry of Education, and the European Social Fund under contract TIN2011-23839 (*"Scriptongue"*). Aldalur has a doctoral grant from the Spanish Ministry of Science & Education.

References

1. Alimadadi, S., Sequeira, S., Mesbah, A., Pattabiraman, K.: Understanding javascript event-based interactions. In: ICSE 2013 (2013)
2. Daniel, F., Matera, M.: Mashups - Concepts, Models and Architectures. Data-Centric Systems and Applications. Springer, Heidelberg (2014)
3. Díaz, O., Arellano, C.: The augmented web: rationales, opportunities, and challenges on browser-side transcoding. TWEB **9**(2), 8 (2015)
4. Díaz, O., Arellano, C., Aldalur, I., Medina, H., Firmenich, S.: End-user browser-side modification of web pages. In: Benatallah, B., Bestavros, A., Manolopoulos, Y., Vakali, A., Zhang, Y. (eds.) WISE 2014, Part I. LNCS, vol. 8786, pp. 293–307. Springer, Heidelberg (2014)
5. Dzwinel, K.: SnappySnippet (2013). https://github.com/kdzwinel/SnappySnippet
6. Florentin. HtmlClipper (2010). http://www.betterprogramming.com/htmlclipper.html
7. Maras, J., Stula, M., Carlson, J., Crnkovic, I.: Identifying code of individual features in client-side web applications. IEEE Trans. Softw. Eng. **39**(12), 1680–1697 (2013)
8. Melnyk, V., Ashok, V., Puzis, Y., Soviak, A., Borodin, Y., Ramakrishnan, I.V.: Widget classification with applications to web accessibility. In: Casteleyn, S., Rossi, G., Winckler, M. (eds.) ICWE 2014. LNCS, vol. 8541, pp. 341–358. Springer, Heidelberg (2014)
9. Safi, W., Maurel, F., Routoure, J., Beust, P., Dias, G.: Hybrid segmentation of web pages for vibro-tactile access on touch-screen devices. In: ICWE 2014, DC (2014)
10. W3C. Packaged Web Apps (Widgets) (2012). http://www.w3.org/TR/widgets/
11. W3C. Web Components (2013). http://www.w3.org/TR/components-intro/

Mashup Development with Web Liquid Streams

Andrea Gallidabino$^{(\boxtimes)}$, Masiar Babazadeh, and Cesare Pautasso

Faculty of Informatics, University of Lugano (USI), Lugano, Switzerland
{andrea.gallidabino,masiar.babazadeh,cesare.pautasso}@usi.ch

Abstract. Web services such as Twitter and Facebook provide direct
access to their streaming APIs. The data generated by all of their users
is forwarded in quasi-real-time to any external client requesting it: this
continuous feed opens up new ways to create mashups that differ from
existing data aggregation approaches, which focus on presenting with
multiple widgets an integrated view of the data that is pulled from multiple sources. Streaming data flows directly into the mashup without the
need to fetch it in advance, making it possible to exchange data between
mashup components through streaming channels. In this challenge submission we show how streaming APIs can be integrated using a stream
processing framework. Mashup components can be seen as stream operators, while the mashup can be defined by building a streaming topology.
The mashup is built with Web Liquid Streams, a dynamic streaming
framework that takes advantage of standard Web protocols to deploy
stream topologies both on Web servers and Web browsers.

Keywords: Mashups · Streaming · Liquid Software

1 Introduction

The mashup concept and the interest in the mashup tools started to appear when
more and more Web services and Web Data sources were released [1]. While
mashups can be built using traditional Web development tools, languages and
frameworks, specialized mashup composition tools have appeared focusing on
raising the level of abstraction and thus enabling non-programmers to compose
mashups [2]. Different tools can be characterized depending on the users they
target, and the mashup development approach they implement [3]. A precise
categorisation of the various mashup tools describes synthetically their expressive
power and the type of solution they propose can be found in [4].

Mashups are in general data centric applications which gather data from
many Web services or Web data sources and mix them together in a single integrated application. Data may be fetched from the Web in many different forms:
static resources accessible through static URLs (e.g. JSON/XML files), resources
accessible through REST APIs, or – in the case of this paper – streaming and
feed APIs that forward new data to clients without the need of any new request
after the initial subscription. Mashup tools make it easy to integrate one or more
of those type of data.

© Springer International Publishing Switzerland 2016
F. Daniel and C. Pautasso (Eds.): RMC 2015, CCIS 591, pp. 98–117, 2016.
DOI: 10.1007/978-3-319-28727-0_7

This paper presents the rapid mashup challenge solution proposed by the Web Liquid Streams (WLS) framework [5], a stream processing runtime that helps developers deploy streaming topologies running on heterogeneous Web-enabled devices. WLS helps the users to develop logic mashups by creating JavaScript logic components. Components may interact with any of the data sources described above and components may be connected together in order to create a streaming topology representing the mashup.

2 Related Work

As witnessed during the challenge, there exists many mashup tools based on different paradigms and runtime architectures. By using the Web browser as a platform, many tools implement the logic of both the **integration** and the **presentation** directly on the Web browser. While the presentation layer suits perfectly the Web browser environment, there are some issues with the integration layer, which can not always be fully deployed on the Web browser [6]. The solution to this problem is decoupling the integration and presentation layer by shifting the development of mashup from the client-side to the server-side [7]. With Web Liquid Streams, it is possible to dynamically decide where mashup components should be deployed.

Many mashup tools take advantage of the data flow paradigm to represent how information and events flow between mashup components connected into pipelines. Tools like *FeedsAPI*[1], *Superpipes*[2], or *Yahoo Pipes*[3] use pipelines as a mechanism for developing mashups. The idea is to create a **flow** of data that goes from a multitude of sources through one or many integration layers and finally ends the flow in the presentation layer.

The pipeline approach can be easily implemented in a streaming framework [8] because all the layers of a pipelined mashup can be directly translated to a type of operator in a streaming topology: data sources used in a mashup translate to *producer* operators, the integration layers translate to *filter* operators, and the presentation layer translates to *consumer* operators. Even if streaming frameworks naturally suit the implementation of pipelines, not all streaming frameworks are suited for mashup development. Mashup development with streaming frameworks must meet two criteria: operators must be able to interact with external data sources and Web APIs and there must be a mechanism enabling visualisation of the consumer operators and their deployment as Web Widgets.

JOpera is a process-based [9] mashup composition tool that was extended in 2009 with streaming execution support to build real-time mashups of stream data sources found on the Web [10].

---

[1] http://www.feedsapi.com/.
[2] https://github.com/superfeedr/superpipes.
[3] https://pipes.yahoo.com/pipes/.

Chrooma+ [11] is a streaming mashup tool that enables construction of mashups with video and audio sources. It can create composition of media streams with any HTML component.

SensorMasher [12] uses streams of data produced by sensors as data sources and builds visual compositions on a Web browser. SensorMasher publishes the data of the attached sensors as Web data sources, making it possible to integrate them with other data sources.

3   Web Liquid Streams Framework

WLS helps Web developers to create streaming topologies running across heterogeneous Web-enabled devices. Any device on which a Web browser or a node.js Web server can run, can be used to produce, process or consume a WLS stream. WLS targets programmers that are able to write JavaScript code that runs both on the server and on the client. Mashup components in WLS are called *operators* and may interact with any Web service API (both streaming, RESTful and RPC-based). An operator is the core building block of a streaming topology, it can receive data, process it and forward results downstream. By *binding* (connecting) two or more operators together it is possible to define a streaming topology.

Operators may run on Web servers or on Web browsers. In both environments they can use the same WLS API to produce and consume the data stream (see Sect. 3.4). Operators running on a Web Browser also have access to an extended API for rendering the data stream and visualize it on web pages (see Sect. 3.5). Figure 1 shows the scheme of a possible topology composed by three operators: the producer and filter run in the server-side while the producer runs on a browser. In this example the filter makes requests to an external API.

WLS abstracts away the deployment on the heterogeneous machines from the development of the topology. It keeps the mashup alive in case of failures. If a mashup component overload is detected it automatically allocates more resources to that component [13].

In this section we discuss the features offered in the WLS framework in more detail. Explanations are followed by real examples used in the demo.

3.1   Startup and Discovery of the Devices

Discovery of the devices happens by direct connection through different entry points provided by the WLS runtime. When WLS finishes the initialisation, a list of ports is prompted on the screen (Fig. 2). Every port defines a specific entry point or a service published by the WLS application. Smart devices running the WLS-node script can connect to the application by connecting to the *RCP* entry point, while Web browser enabled peers can connect to the *Remote* entry point. Through the *HTTP* port it is possible to send HTTP requests.

WLS also publishes a RESTful API [14] through the *REST API ROOT* port. During the demo we show how to retrieve topology descriptions through this interface (Fig. 9).

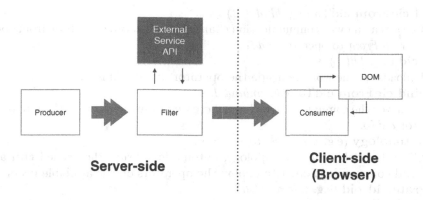

Fig. 1. Web Liquid Streams topology example

```
andrea@neha:~/usi_liquid_streams$ DEBUG=wls:root node koala_root 10088
  wls:root HTTP server listening on port 10087 +0ms
  wls:root RPC server listening on port 10088 +7ms
  wls:root Service up and running +2ms
  wls:root spawning node using port = 10088 +0ms
  wls:root REMOTE server listening on port: 10085 +4ms
  wls:root host: neha.inf.unisi.ch port: 10091 #processors: 48 cpu usage: 0 +1s
  wls:root REST API ROOT listening on port 10086 +29ms
```

Fig. 2. Web Liquid Streams startup

When devices connect to the WLS application they become *Peers* and an unique peer id (*pid*) is assigned to them. Figure 3 shows the WLS application's answer to the connection of one server peer and three remote peers connected through a Web browser.

```
andrea@neha:~/usi_liquid_streams$ DEBUG=wls:root:connected node koala_root 10088
  wls:root:connected New node connected: (id:0, alias:N0, host:neha.inf.unisi.ch) +0ms
  wls:root:connected New remote node connected: (id:1, alias:B1) +5s
  wls:root:connected New remote node connected: (id:2, alias:B2) +2s
  wls:root:connected New remote node connected: (id:3, alias:B3) +2s
```

Fig. 3. Web Liquid Streams discovery

3.2 Commands

WLS provides a list of console commands allowing live development of a mashup:

run script pid (e.g. *run producer.js 1*)

Creates a new operator on peer *pid* and loads the defined *script*. Workers inside the operator will run the loaded script. The *run* command returns a unique operator identifier (*cid*) representing the created operator.

bind cidFrom cidTo (e.g. *bind 1 2*)

Creates a one-way communication channel between two operators: from operator *cidFrom* to operator *cidTo*.

kill cid (e.g. *kill 1*)

Unloads all the workers inside the operator *cid* and kills it.

unbind cidFrom cidTo (e.g. *unbind 1 2*)

Removes the communication channel created from operator *cidFrom* to operator *cidTo*.

exec topology (e.g. *exec icwe_topology.js*)

Given the definition of a topology, automatically runs the needed **run** and **bind** commands in order to deploy the operators on the available peers.

migrate cid pid (e.g. *migrate 1 0*)

Move operator *cid* from its current peer to peer *pid*.

Figure 4 shows a real example of running and binding operators. Two operators are run with scripts *icwe_producer.js* and *icwe_f1.js* on pid 0. The run command returns two *cid*: the runtime assigns to the first operator cid 0 and to the second one cid 1. When both operators are started it is possible to bind them with the bind command.

```
andrea@neha:~/usi_liquid_streams$ DEBUG=wls:node:*,wls:command node koala_root 10088
run icwe_producer.js 0
  wls:node:runc Running worker with uid = 0 +0ms
  wls:command done: 0 +0ms
run icwe_f1.js 0
  wls:node:runc Running worker with uid = 1 +13s
  wls:command done: 1 +13s
bind 0 1
  wls:node:bindc node bind cluster 0 -> 1 +9s
  wls:command done: binding done in cid 0 to cid 1 +9s
```

Fig. 4. Running and binding example

3.3 Topology

A topology can be described with our internal DSL based on the JSON syntax[4]. The description defines both *operators* and *bindings* as follows:

operators

id Identifier of the operator

script Script loaded in the operator and ran by the workers

browser Defines if an operator may run on the client-side, if not defined the operator exists exclusively on the server-side

path Relative path of the domain that enables direct access to the operator through a Web browser connection

---

[4] http://json.org/.

only If *true* an operator runs exclusively on the client-side, if *false* the operator may run on both server-side and client-side

bindings

from Identifier of an operator defined in the operator array

to Identifier of an operator defined in the operator array

type Sending algorithm such as: *round-robin* or *broadcast*

Listing 1.1 shows the implementation of a linear topology composed by three operators: the first and second operators can run only on the server-side, while the third one can run only in a browser and is accessible to the URL */map*. The first operator sends messages to the second one in a round-robin fashion, the second broadcasts messages to the third one.

Listing 1.1. Topology JSON description example: linear topology with three operators used in the first iteration of the demo

```
 1  {
 2       "topology": {
 3            "id": "test",
 4            "operators": [{
 5                    "id": "producer",
 6                    "script": "icwe_producer.js"
 7                },{
 8                    "id": "filter",
 9                    "script": "icwe_f1.js"
10                },{
11                    "id": "consumer",
12                    "script": "icwe_browser.js",
13                    "browser": {
14                        "path" : "/map",
15                        "only" : true
16                    }
17                }
18            ],
19            "bindings": [{
20                    "from": "producer",
21                    "to": "filter",
22                    "type": "round_robin"
23                },{
24                    "from": "filter",
25                    "to": "consumer",
26                    "type": "broadcast"
27                }
28            ]
29       }
30  }
```

3.4   Script API

WLS provides developers with the following basic API:

var wls = require('wls.js')

An operator script has to import the *WLS* library. The library contains the two streaming routines needed to create the topology's streaming flow. Our framework redefines the *require* function in the remote clients in order to make server-side scripts and client-side scripts as compatible as possible without the need of any further modification. It is important to note that in the **client-side** the *require* function should be called only once in order to load the WLS library, since it always returns the *WLS* object no matter the arguments passed (it does not load any server-side node modules).

wls.createOperator(function(message){ ... })

The *createOperator* method is used to execute scripts on messages coming from upstream. It takes a **callback** function parameter which is executed every time a message is parsed by the operator. The callback function receives the *message* itself as the first argument. A script can define only a single operator.

wls.send(message)

The *send* method is used to send messages downstream to all operators bound to the sender. The message must be a serializable object. We highly recommend to send JSON parsable objects as messages.

Listing 1.2 shows the implementation of one of the scripts used in the rapid mashup challenge (Sect. 4). The script receives a message from upstream as an argument to the callback registered with *wls.createOperator* (lines 4–8). When processing every stream message, the script makes an external HTTP request in the *geoNamesRequest* function (lines 10–25). The answer to the request is eventually forwarded downstream through the *wls.send* function (lines 18–22).

Listing 1.2. Server script: Tweet Geolocate

```
1   var wls = require('wls.js')
2   var http = require('http')
3
4   wls.createOperator(function(msg) {
5       var tweet = msg.tweet
6       var locationName = getLocationName(tweet)
7       geoNamesRequest(locationName, tweet)
8   })
9
10  var geoNamesRequest = function(locationName, tweet){
11      var options = {...}
12
13      http.get(options, function(res) {
14          var coords = undefined
15          ...
16
```

```
17              res.on('end', function () {
18                  wls.send({
19                      tweet: tweet,
20                      color: createRandomColor(),
21                      location: coords
22                  })
23              })
24          })
25  }
26  // Returns the name of a location connected to the tweet
27  var getLocationName = function (tweet) {...}
28  // Returns a random color
29  var createRandomColor = function () {...}
```

3.5 Extended Remote Script API

Implementation of WLS in the Web browser is slightly different from the server-side. Workers in the server-side are spawned as child-processes of the WLS runtime, while in the Web browser workers run as WebWorkers. Scripts running in a Web browser should be able to access and interact with the Document Object Model (*DOM*) of the Web page, but WebWorkers lack direct access to the DOM. The remote peers in the browsers have access to an extended set of API methods that enhance the communication between the *DOM* and the operator's script.

wls.createHTML(id, html)
    The *createHTML* method adds HTML code snippets to the DOM. It takes two parameters: a unique *id* and the HTML code snippet passed as a String.
wls.createScript(id, scriptPath)
    The *createScript* method adds a client-side script to the header of the associated Web page. It takes two parameters: a unique *id* and the path to the script relative to the domain name.
wls.callFunction(name, argumentsArray [, function(result){...}])
    The *callFunction* method calls a function associated to the *DOM* from within the WebWorker. If the *DOM* defines a function named *name*, then it will be executed by passing the *argumentsArray* as the arguments. If the optional callback function is passed as an argument, it will be executed after the function call ends. The callback takes the returned value of the executed function as the first parameter.
wls.setDOM(selector, attribute, value)
    The *setDOM* method sets a new *value* to the *attribute* of the specified *DOM* elements. The elements are specified by the *selector* parameter and are written as *jQuery selectors*[5].
wls.subscribe(id)
    The *subscribe* method creates a direct communication channel from the *DOM* to the WebWorker. Once the WebWorkers subscribe, the *DOM* can create

---

[5] https://api.jquery.com/category/selectors/.

and send messages to the WebWorkers as if the *DOM* is an operator in the topology. It can send messages through the channels with the framework function **WLS.publish(id, message)**, where *id* is the unique identifier specified in the *subscribe* call and *message* is the object forwarded by the *DOM*.

Listings 1.3, 1.5, and 1.6 show the implementation of the three remote scripts used in the rapid mashup challenge (Sect. 4).

In Listing 1.3 we show the script that creates markers inside the GoogleMap. The first time the script is loaded it will inject the GoogleMap HTML into the DOM by using the function *wls.createHTML* (line 7) and it will inject into the header of the Web page the script 'js/map.js' (Listing 1.4) by using the function *wls.createScript* (line 8). When a message arrives from upstream (lines 1–6) the message is processed and the worker will call the *addMarker* function which is now defined in the DOM by using the *wls.callFunction* method.

In Listing 1.5 we show the script that visualises information associated to the markers on the GoogleMap. The first time the script is loaded it registers a new subscriber by calling the *wls.subscribe* method (line 9). Whenever in the DOM the method *WLS.publish('markermouseover', msg)* is called (Listing 1.4: line 8–10), a message is forwarded to the worker script, as if it had received a message from upstreams (lines 2–8). Once the message is processed, the script will modify some attributes of the Web page by calling the *wls.setDOM* method (lines 5–7).

Similarly in Listing 1.6 the script registers a subscriber called *markerclick* (line 9). Wherever the DOM calls the method *WLS.publish('markerclick', msg)* (Listing 1.4: line 4–6) a message is sent to the worker script.

Listing 1.3. Browser Script: Marker Creator

```
1  wls . createOperator ( function ( msg ) {
2      var tweet = msg . tweet
3      var color = msg . color
4      var location = msg . location
5      wls . callFunction ( 'addMarker' ,[ tweet , color , location ],
           undefined )
6  })
7  wls . createHTML ( 'mapDiv' , '<div id="map - canvas"></div>' );
8  wls . createScript ( 'mapScript' , 'js/map . js' );
```

Listing 1.4. js/map.js script

```
1  var addMarker = function ( tweet , color , location ) {
2      ...
3
4      google . maps . event . addListener ( marker , 'click' , function (){
5          WLS . publish ( 'markerclick' , { tweet : tweet , color : color ,
               count : count })
6      }
7      ...
8      google . maps . event . addListener ( marker , 'mouseover' , function (){
```

```
9          WLS.publish('markermouseover', {tweet:tweet, color:color
                })
10     }
11     ...
12  }
```

Listing 1.5. Browser Script: Marker Viewer

```
1  var wls = require('wls.js')
2  wls.createOperator(function(msg) {
3      var tweet = msg.tweet
4      var color = msg.color
5      wls.setDOM('#marker_color', 'css', "background-color", color
            )
6      wls.setDOM('#marker_author', 'html', tweet.user.screen_name)
7      wls.setDOM('#marker_tweet', 'html', tweet.text)
8  })
9  wls.subscribe('markermouseover')
10 wls.createHTML(...);
```

Listing 1.6. Browser Script: Marker Clicker

```
1  var wls = require('wls.js')
2  wls.createOperator(function(msg) {
3      wls.send({
4          tweet: msg.tweet,
5          color: msg.color,
6          count: msg.count
7      })
8  })
9  wls.subscribe('markerclick')
```

4   Rapid Mashup Challenge

Figure 5 summarizes the final topology deployed during the demo, the description of the scripts can be found in Sect. 4.2. The mashup we propose in the demo mixes the following three external APIs:

Geonames
Geonames[6] converts name Strings to a pair of latitude-longitude coordinates. Answers from the GeoNames API are in JSON format, which can be forwarded downstream without the need of any processing.

GoogleMaps
GoogleMaps[7] adds a geographic map to a Web page, its API allows creation of markers on the map given the latitude-longitude coordinates.

---

[6] http://www.geonames.org/.
[7] https://developers.google.com/maps/.

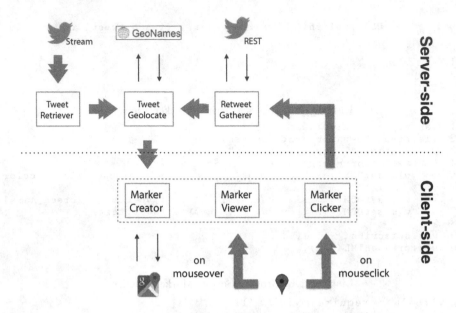

Fig. 5. Complete stream topology and component deployment

Twitter REST API[8] and Streaming API[9]

 REST: The Twitter REST API is used to retrieve all the re-tweets associated to a given tweet.

 Streaming: We subscribe to the streaming feed of *The New York Times* (TNYT) Twitter account *@nytimes*. Every time The New York Times tweets a piece of news, a message is forwarded to our operator.

The rapid mashup challenge demo mashup marks on a map the geographical location of the news published by *The New York Times*. Moreover the mashup detects two different events associated to the marker: when the mouse is over a marker the mashup returns additional textual information about the news; when a marker is clicked it shows on the map, with smaller markers of the same color, the geographical location of all the users who retweeted it.

During the challenge we incrementally build the mashup from scratch, starting with the definition of a simple linear topology with our JSON syntax. The initial topology only shows the tweets on the GoogleMap.

After the initial solution, we expand the topology dynamically by invoking the console commands described in Sect. 3.2. The extended topology is now non-linear, it re-uses the *Tweet Geolocate* component, and offers the *onclick* and *mouseover* functionalities. The extended mashup has been obtained by incrementally adding components to it without stopping its execution, a form of live mashup development [15].

---

[8] https://dev.twitter.com/rest/public.
[9] https://dev.twitter.com/streaming/overview.

At the end of the demo we ask the audience to connect to our Web application. Anybody that connects to the mashup with his Web browser will be able to see the GoogleMap. With the new clients connected to WLS we demonstrate the migration and the distribution of the mashup components over the set of peers contributed by the audience.

4.1 Motivation

The proposed mashup allows the demonstration of the most important features offered by WLS:

Topology definition. Topologies can be created by the means of our DSL language and executed automatically.

Live mashup development. Topologies can be extended at runtime and components can be added or removed while already existing mashups are running.

Reusable components. Components are independent from the topology they were created for. The *Tweet Geolocate* is used both in the initial topology and the extended one with different upstreams operators.

Distributed user interface mashups. The live demo shows that more than one operator can be instantiated to visualise the data. The stream topology can be deployed on different clients and therefore its results are shared among multiple users.

4.2 Scripts

The rapid mashup challenge is composed by three server-side scripts and three client-side scripts.

4.2.1 Server-Side

Tweet Retriever. The operator subscribes to the feed of 'The New York Times' Twitter. When a new tweet is forwarded to the operator it is processed and trimmed of the useless data. The processed tweet is forwarded to the *Tweet Geolocate* operator.

Tweet Geolocate. The implementation of this operator can be found in Listing 1.2. The Twitter feed does not directly return the latitude-longitude coordinates of the news. This operator searches for a location name inside the tweet and sends an HTTP request to the GeoNames API. The tweet and the GeoNames answer is **broadcasted** downstream to all *Marker Creator* operators.

Re-tweet Gatherer. The operator receives a tweet and a number from upstream. It sends an HTTP request to the REST Twitter API and requests the first n re-tweets connected to the given tweet, where n is the number received from upstream. Every single retweet is then forwarded in a message to the *Tweet Geolocate* operator.

4.2.2   Client-Side

Marker Creator. The implementation of this operator script can be found in Listing 1.3. This operator injects the HTML code and javascript of the GoogleMap into the Web page. Every time a tweet arrives from upstreams it calls a function defined in the DOM which adds a marker on the GoogleMap. Figure 6 shows the map on the Web page with some markers on it. Big markers are news tweeted by the TNYT, while small markers are retweets.

Marker Viewer. The implementation of this operator script can be found in Listing 1.5. This script adds an HTML tweet viewer to the Web page (Fig. 7). When the *mouseover* event of a marker is fired the operator receives the tweet as a stream message and changes the page accordingly by showing the most relevant information on the Web page: marker color, author, and text of the tweet.

Marker Clicker. The implementation of this operator script can be found in Listing 1.6. This script adds a number picker to the Web page. When the *click* event of a marker is fired the operator receives a message with the tweet and the number selected in the picker. The operator sends a request downstream to the *Retweet Gatherer* with both information.

Fig. 6. Marker Creator

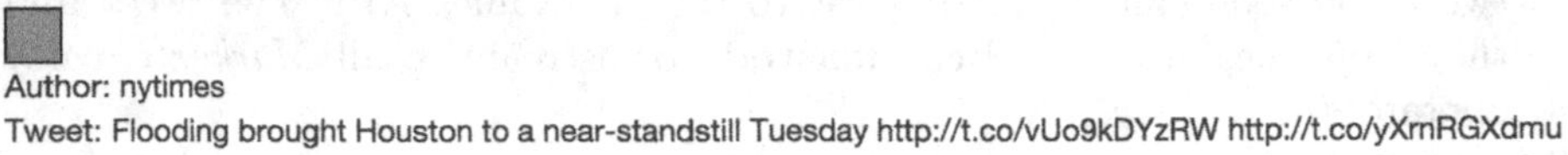

Author: nytimes
Tweet: Flooding brought Houston to a near-standstill Tuesday http://t.co/vUo9kDYzRW http://t.co/yXrnRGXdmu

Fig. 7. Marker Viewer

5   Demo

We present our plan for the rapid mashup challenge with a five-phase demo.
Scripts are defined in advance and are not discussed during the challenge demonstration.

5.1   Slides Presentation

The slides presentation[10] gives the audience a general introduction to WLS. The
presentation describes the concept of *operators*, *binding*, and *topology*. Moreover
it presents the console commands used during the demo: *run*, *bind*, *exec*, and
migrate. Lastly it introduces the JSON description of a topology and the possibility to dynamically change it at runtime.

5.2   Startup and Connection

We open the demo by starting the application and explaining the console log
messages (see Sect. 3.1). In particular we not only show the audience the different
ports and services, but specifically the connection of the peers. We explain that
the server itself is a peer and the application assigns pid *0* to it.

Afterwards we open a Web browser (Chrome or Firefox) and connect to the
framework through the *remote* port. The console logs the connection of a new
remote peer and assigns the pid *1* to it.

At this point the set of peers managed by the application consists of two
peers: a server with pid *0* and a remote peer with pid *1*.

5.3   Topology Creation and Deployment

We create the JSON description of a linear topology. The topology is created
on a text editor so that people can see the description of the *operators* and
bindings. We construct the topology iteratively allowing the audience to connect
what they see with what they heard during the slides presentation.

We use an empty JSON template (Listing 1.7) as a starting point for the
creation. After briefly explaining the template we add the three operators *Tweet
Retriever*, *Tweet Geolocate*, and *Marker Creator*. In particular we make sure to
explain the audience that the first two operators will run on the server while the
last one will run on a Web browser by defining the *browser* flag (see Sect. 3.3).

Lastly we add to the description two bindings connecting the three operators,
making sure to explain the difference between the *round-robin* and *broadcast*
sending algorithm. The final topology description can be viewed in Listing 1.1.

---

[10] http://www.slideshare.net/AndreaGallidabino/web-liquid-streams-mashup-challenge-icwe-2015.

Listing 1.7. Topology description starting point

```
1  {
2      "topology": {
3          "id": "test",
4          "operators": [
5              "ADD OPERATORS HERE"
6          ],
7          "bindings": [
8              "ADD BINDINGS HERE"
9          ]
10     }
11 }
```

After the definition of the JSON file we can execute the topology. We remind the audience about the console commands and call *exec*. The console prompts messages as if it had executed three *run* commands and two *bind* commands (see Sect. 3.2). Figure 8 shows the view created on the Web browser: it shows the pid *1* on the top, the GoogleMap and the cid *2* which is the same operator identifier written on the console (meaning that the GoogleMap was added to the Web page by the *Marker Creator* operator).

PID: 1

CID: 2

Fig. 8. First Iteration: News Stream on the Map

Then we show that by connecting to the *REST API* port (see Sect. 3.1), we can see the current topology ran by the application. Figure 9 shows the extended JSON description displayed on the Web browser. This description has many more fields than the one described previously because it also contains information about the runtime of the operators (such as the *cpu_usage* or *workers*).

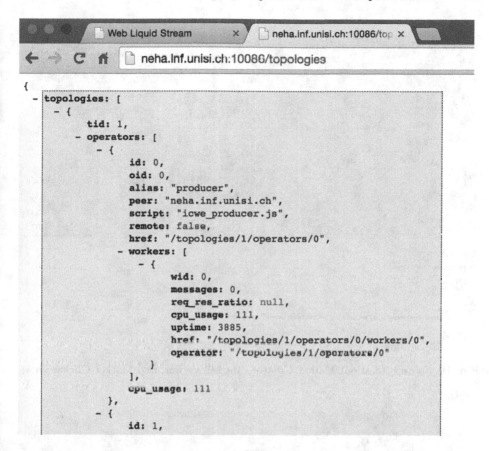

```
{
  - topologies: [
    - {
        tid: 1,
        - operators: [
          - {
              id: 0,
              oid: 0,
              alias: "producer",
              peer: "neha.inf.unisi.ch",
              script: "icwe_producer.js",
              remote: false,
              href: "/topologies/1/operators/0",
              - workers: [
                - {
                    wid: 0,
                    messages: 0,
                    req_res_ratio: null,
                    cpu_usage: 111,
                    uptime: 3885,
                    href: "/topologies/1/operators/0/workers/0",
                    operator: "/topologies/1/operators/0"
                  }
              ],
              cpu_usage: 111
            },
          - {
              id: 1,
```

Fig. 9. Topology description retrieved from the REST API

At this point the Web browser displays the map and every time a tweet or retweet arrives to the client operator a randomly colored marker drops on the map.

5.4 Topology Development

We dynamically extend the current topology so that we construct the complete solution to the rapid mashup challenge. We use the console commands *run* for the three scripts *Marker Viewer*, *Marker Clicker*, and *Retweet Gatherer*.

Once the run commands finish their execution we show the changes on the Web browser (Fig. 10). The Web page now contains some new HTML, in particular we see a number picker added by the *Marker Clicker* operator with cid *3* and the tweet viewer added by the *Marker Viewer* operator with cid *4*.

We show that by triggering the *mouseover* event on a marker the *Tweet Viewer* HTML changes accordingly, while if we try to trigger the *click* event nothing happens. We explain to the audience what is missing, i.e. the fact that

PID: 1

CID: 2

Quantity (between 1 and 20): 20

CID: 3

Author: nytimes
Tweet: In busy Silicon Valley, protein powder is in demand http://t.co/2iTaHgsG0d http://t.co/UggF5f5gqr

CID: 4

Fig. 10. Second Iteration: Marker Creator, Marker Viewer, and Marker Clicker views

PID: 1

CID: 2

Quantity (between 1 and 20): 20

CID: 3

Author: nytimes
Tweet: Flooding brought Houston to a near-standstill Tuesday http://t.co/vUo9kDYzRW http://t.co/yXmRGXdmu

CID: 4

Fig. 11. Fully functional rapid mashup challenge

we still did not create the bindings to the *Retweet Gatherer*. We run on the console the two needed *bind* commands, connecting the *Retweet Gatherer* to the *Marker Clicker* and to the *Tweet Geolocate* operators.

Finally we can show the audience that by clicking on a marker in the map the retweets appear. Figure 11 shows the final outcome of the demo on the Web browser: if a tweet (big marker) is clicked, then many retweets (small markers) of the same color appear on the map.

5.5 Live Demo and Migration

We invite the audience to participate in the demo and give them the application URL. They connect to the direct address of the map operator defined in the JSON topology (Listing 1.8). Anybody connecting to the application can see the GoogleMap and receive the markers on their Web browser. We show that we can move the map from one peer to another with the command *migrate* without stopping the runtime.

Listing 1.8. Consumer browser direct access

```
1 {
2     "id": "consumer",
3     "script": "icwe_browser.js",
4     "browser": {
5         "path" : "/map",
6         "only" : true
7     }
8 },
```

6   Conclusions

We presented Web Liquid Streams and how it can be used to develop mashups of streaming Web APIs. Like many data-flow based mashup tools, Web Liquid Streams uses pipelines to represent how information flows between Web data sources and the widgets visualising it. However, Web Liquid Streams data flow pipelines can have arbitrary topology and are used to continuously stream data so that the mashup widgets can be updated in real-time as more information is streamed through the mashup.

WLS runs both on Web servers and Web browser-enabled devices making it possible to implement the presentation layer on the Web browsers and dynamically spread the integration layers between the Web servers and the Web browsers. Moreover any peer attached to the application (i.e. sensors, browsers, ...) can become a Data producer, filter as well as consumer of a topology. During the 10 min of the rapid mashup challenge we demonstrated the main features of the framework: Static deployment of the mashup topology with JSON descriptions, iterative and incremental live development of a topology at runtime and the liquid [16] distribution of the mashup widgets on different Web browsers.

We are currently working on a visual topology editor tool, which would shift the building of a mashup from the textual editing of low-level JSON descriptions to a high level visual drag-and-drop. The tool would connect and interact with the already implemented REST API of the runtime for monitoring and deployment of the mashup topology.

Acknowledgment. The work is supported by the Hasler Foundation with the Liquid Software Architecture (LiSA) project.

Appendix

Mashup Feature Checklist

Mashup Type	Logic mashups
Component Types	Logic components
Runtime Location	Both Client and Server
Integration Logic	Choreographed integration
Data Passing Logic	Direct data passing
Instantiation Lifecycle	Short-living

Mashup Tool Feature Checklist

Targeted End-User	Programmers
Automation Degree	Semi-automation or manual
Liveness Level	Level 4
Interaction Technique	Textual DSL and other (console)
Online User Community	None

References

1. Zang, N., Rosson, M.B., Nasser, V.: Mashups: who? what? why? In: CHI 2008 Extended Abstracts on Human Factors in Computing Systems, pp. 3171–3176. ACM (2008)
2. Liu, Y., Liang, X., Xu, L., Staples, M., Zhu, L.: Composing enterprise mashup components and services using architecture integration patterns. J. Syst. Softw. **84**(9), 1436–1446 (2011)
3. Aghaee, S., Nowak, M., Pautasso, C.: Reusable decision space for mashup tool design. In: Proceedings of the 4th ACM SIGCHI Symposium on Engineering Interactive Computing Systems, pp. 211–220. ACM (2012)
4. Daniel, F., Matera, M.: Mashups: Concepts, Models and Architectures. Data-Centric Systems and Applications. Springer, Heidelberg (2014)
5. Babazadeh, M., Gallidabino, A., Pautasso, C.: Decentralized stream processing over web-enabled devices. In: Dustdar, S., Leymann, F., Villari, M. (eds.) ESOCC 2015. LNCS, vol. 9306, pp. 3–18. Springer, Heidelberg (2015)

6. Aghaee, S., Pautasso, C.: Mashup development with HTML5. In: 4th International Workshop on Web APIs and Services Mashups (Mashups 2010), Ayia Napa, Cyprus, pp. 10:1–10:8. ACM, December 2010
7. Daniel, F., Matera, M., Yu, J., Benatallah, B., Saint-Paul, R., Casati, F.: Understanding ui integration: a survey of problems, technologies, and opportunities. IEEE Internet Comput. 11(3), 59–66 (2007)
8. Hirzel, M., et al.: A catalog of stream processing optimizations. ACM Comput. Surv. 46(4), 46:1–46:34 (2014)
9. Daniel, F., Koschmider, A., Nestler, T., Roy, M., Namoun, A.: Toward process mashups: key ingredients and open research challenges. In: Proceedings of the 3rd and 4th International Workshop on Web APIs and Services Mashups. Mashups 2009/2010, New York, NY, USA, pp. 9:1–9:8. ACM (2010)
10. Biörnstad, B., Pautasso, C.: Let it flow: building mashups with data processing pipelines. In: Di Nitto, E., Ripeanu, M. (eds.) ICSOC 2007. LNCS, vol. 4907, pp. 15–28. Springer, Heidelberg (2009)
11. Oehme, P., Krug, M., Wiedemann, F., Gaedke, M.: The chrooma+ approach to enrich video content using HTML5. In: Proceedings of the 22nd International Conference on World Wide Web Companion, pp. 479–480 (2013)
12. Phuoc, D.L., Hauswirth, M.: Linked open data in sensor data mashups. In: Proceedings of SSN 2009, CEUR, pp. 1–16 (2009)
13. Babazadeh, M., Gallidabino, A., Pautasso, C.: Liquid stream processing across web browsers and web servers. In: Cimiano, P., Frasincar, F., Houben, G.-J., Schwabe, D. (eds.) ICWE 2015. LNCS, vol. 9114, pp. 24–33. Springer, Heidelberg (2015)
14. Babazadeh, M., Pautasso, C.: A restful api for controlling dynamic streaming topologies. In: Proceedings of the Companion Publication of the 23rd International Conference on World Wide Web Companion, International World Wide Web Conferences Steering Committee, pp. 965–970 (2014)
15. Aghaee, S., Pautasso, C.: Live mashup tools: challenges and opportunities. In: 2013 1st International Workshop on Live Programming (LIVE), pp. 1–4 IEEE (2013)
16. Mikkonnen, T., Systa, K., Pautasso, C.: Towards liquid web applications. In: Cimiano, P., Frasincar, F., Houben, G.-J., Schwabe, D. (eds.) ICWE 2015. LNCS, vol. 9114, pp. 134–143. Springer, Heidelberg (2015)

Challenge Outcome and Conclusion

Cesare Pautasso[1] and Florian Daniel[2]([⊠])

[1] Faculty of Informatics, University of Lugano (USI), Lugano, Switzerland
`cesare.pautasso@usi.ch`
[2] University of Trento, Via Sommarive 9, 38123 Povo, TN, Italy
`daniel@disi.unitn.it`

Abstract. In the following we report on the outcome of the ICWE 2015 Rapid Mashup Challenge (RMC), describe the voting system used, and draw some conclusions regarding the presented works.

Keywords: Mashups · Challenge · Benchmarking

1 Challenge Organization

We recall that every tool participating in the challenge was allocated 10 min for a short presentation with the goal to introduce the tool, illustrate its design and enumerate its most important features. Some participants also used the time to present the mashup to be built and discuss their choice of required Web APIs to be mashed up with others they could freely choose and how they were going to use their tool to assemble the mashup.

The demo part was also 10 min long, during which the mashup was developed in front of the audience. The starting point for all demos was an empty workspace in which the components to be used in the mashup had been pre-registered and pre-defined, but not yet assembled. Some authors chose to follow an iterative process, whereby the mashup was grown incrementally, piece by piece. Others also included a more general overview of the mashup tool capabilities, which was useful to demonstrate the expressive power of the tool, but did not necessarily help them build the most impressive mashup during the allocated time frame.

Each time a mashup was complete and the time for the demonstration had expired, the jury and audience had the opportunity to ask questions to the authors. This short interactive session had not been originally planned, but was very useful to provide the mashup authors with valuable feedback. During the same time, the challenge evaluation was collected through the ASQ system. The results were aggregated and the challenge ranking updated and shown to the audience and the tool authors.

2 The ASQ Voting System

The challenge evaluation phase was supported by the ASQ system [1]. ASQ (a permutation over Slides-Questions-Answers) allows anyone with a Web browser to

© Springer International Publishing Switzerland 2016
F. Daniel and C. Pautasso (Eds.): RMC 2015, CCIS 591, pp. 118–122, 2016.
DOI: 10.1007/978-3-319-28727-0_8

follow a slideshow presentation and interact with the content by answering questions embedded in the slides. It was originally developed at the USI Faculty of Informatics to support in-classroom teaching activities by taking advantage of the fact that every student comes with his/her laptop to follow the lectures. Students not only can better read the content broadcast to their devices, but teachers can get real-time feedback about their level of understanding and thus adapt their pace and explanation depth during the lecture.

As such ASQ is a general tool and can be used also for any interactive presentation. In particular for the RMC, ASQ was extended with the following features:

- A special question type to gather ratings, over a 5-star scale, with the possibility to award also half stars.
- A count-down timer activated at the beginning of each demonstration to ensure every participant demonstrates his/her tool during the same amount of time.

The intention of introducing ASQ during the RMC was to broaden participation in the evaluation of the challenge participants from the jury to the whole audience (including the authors themselves, who did however not vote in their own turn). A secondary goal was to automate and increase the efficiency of the scoring process, where the answers are aggregated and the final ranking is recomputed after every participant is evaluated. Additionally, the slides showing the metadata about the current participants were interleaved with the questions to evaluate them. This helped to focus the jury's and audience's attention and build a shared awareness of the proceedings of the challenge and manage the time without introducing unnecessary delays.

3   Evaluation Criteria

In line with the call for participation of the RMC, every demonstration was evaluated according to four different criteria:

1. *Mashup Idea.* This focused on the functionality of the mashup to be assembled in under ten minutes. Also it took into account how the authors choose to combine the required APIs with others, if at all. The usefulness of the mashup also would come into play concerning this criteria.
2. *Mashup Complexity.* Given the strict time limit of 10 min, the complexity of the mashup is the challenging aspect. How complex can a mashup actually be when built in such a short time? This criteria was added also to measure the difficulty of building the envisioned mashup idea.
3. *Mashup Solution Elegance.* This criteria shifts the focus to the mashup implementation in the context of the specific mashup tool. The elegance, simplicity and understandability of the resulting mashup solution are all very important aspects that should not be underestimated, despite the emphasis we gave to the speed with which the solution has been assembled.

4. *Tool Power*. Based on the demonstration of the tool, seen in action for 10 min to build a specific mashup, the audience could also reflect on their impression of the tool's expressive power. Thus, this criteria does not reflect a complete analysis of the features of a given tool, but only what could be demonstrated in the limited time available.

4   Results

Table 1 summarizes the feedback obtained from the jury and the audience for each of the tools participating in the challenge in order of presentation.

Table 1. Feedback gathered from the jury/audience during the challenge

Tool	Mashup Idea	Mashup Complexity	Mashup Solution Elegance	Tool Power	Number of Votes
FlexMash	3.35	3.54	3.15	2.92	13
UI-Oriented Computing	3.07	2.57	3.18	2.36	14
SmartComposition	2.79	2.79	2.61	2.79	14
EFESTO	3.29	3.36	3.29	3.82	14
WebMakeup	2.61	2.21	2.64	2.96	14
WLS	3.07	2.90	2.70	3.10	15

Overall, the range of points collected by the tools is rather narrow, from 2.21 (the Mashup Complexity of WebMakeup) to 3.82 (the Tool Power of EFESTO). This shows that the audience – from a minimum of 13 to a maximum of 15 people provided feedback – provided a set of varied ratings, and that there is still room left for improvement in all criteria.

Concerning the Mashup Idea criterion, the tool ranked highest was Flex-Mash (3.35), which also scored highest (3.54) in the Mashup Complexity criteria. EFESTO, on the other hand, was ranked first according to both the Mashup Solution Elegance (3.29) and Tool Power (3.82) criteria.

Combining all criteria with equal weights led to the final ranking in Table 2, according to which EFESTO was awarded the first place in the ICWE 2015 Rapid Mashup Challenge.

5   Limitations

Given the wide variety of approaches to mashup tool design, both from research and industry, and the lack of standard or commonly accepted benchmarks to assess development tools, it remains difficult to give a fair comparison of mashup development tools. To provide an as representative picture as possible of the state of the art in mashup development, the RMC was intentionally left open concerning the type of tool admitted and challenged instead the participants

Table 2. Ranking of the tools participating in the 2015 Rapid Mashup Challenge

Position	Tool	Total score
1	EFESTO [2]	13.75
2	FlexMash [3]	12.96
3	WLS [4]	11.77
4	UI-Oriented Computing [5]	11.18
5	SmartComposition [6]	10.96
6	WebMakeup [7]	10.48

with the rapidity of mashup assembly as the main constraint to compare the tools.

During the challenge, tools were demonstrated by their own authors, something that may invalidate any claim of usability or accessibility, especially by end-user programmers, usually associated with mashup tools. However, since every tool was used by the corresponding authors, the fairness of the comparison is not affected.

Concerning the use of the Web APIs, the second constraint of the challenge, Table 3 shows which APIs were used by each tool. The required APIs were announced one month in advance, giving the authors plenty of time to prepare. If one would want to stress the ability of tools to integrate heterogeneous Web APIs, components and data sources, this time could be reduced while increasing the number of required components in future editions of the challenge.

Table 3. Web APIs composed during the challenge by each mashup tool

Tool	score
FlexMash	NYT, Twitter
UI-Oriented Computing	NYT, Discover Magazine, Yandex Translate
SmartComposition	NYT RSS, AlchemyAPI, YouTube Search, TextTrack, Google Maps, Twitter, Wikipedia, Google Images
EFESTO	Song Kick, YouTube, Vimeo, Google Maps, Google Images
WebMakeup	NYT, NBC News, Google Search, Visual Economy
WLS	Twitter, Google Maps, GeoNames

6   Outlook

Concluding, we consider this first edition of the Rapid Mashup Challenge a success, from the point of view of both the quality of the presented mashup approaches (and authors) and from the number of participants overall to the event (about 30 people throughout the whole event). While on the one hand we have to register that comparing approaches for mashup development that are very different and diverse in their features is intricate and nontrivial, on the other hand, we also have to acknowledge that it is exactly this diversity and the distinguishing features that make the comparison (and the Challenge) interesting. So, the challenge for the future editions of the Challenge – and the process we wanted to start with this first edition of the Challenge – is to identify the right benchmarking approach for mashup tools, while staying open to all kinds of approaches the research community may come up with. This obviously represents a long-term objective, to be achieved over multiple iterations.

The next edition of the Rapid Mashup Challenge will take place at the 16th International Conference on Web Engineering (ICWE2016) next June 9th, 2016 in Lugano, Switzerland.

Acknowledgment. We would like to thank the participants for their enthusiasm and the jury and audience for their active help with the evaluation of the presented approaches. We would also like to thank Vasileios Triglianos for his help and support with the ASQ tool.

References

1. Triglianos, V., Pautasso, C.: Interactive scalable lectures with ASQ. In: Casteleyn, S., Rossi, G., Winckler, M. (eds.) ICWE 2014. LNCS, vol. 8541, pp. 515–518. Springer, Heidelberg (2014)
2. Desolda, G., Ardito, C., Matera, M.: EFESTO: a platform for the end-user development of interactive. In: Daniel, F., Pautasso, C. (eds.) RMC 2015, CCIS 591, pp. 63–81. Springer, Heidelberg (2015)
3. Hirmer, P., Mitschang, B.: FlexMash flexible data mashups based on pattern-based model. In: Daniel, F., Pautasso, C. (eds.) RMC 2015, CCIS 591, pp. 12–30. Springer, Heidelberg (2015)
4. Gallidabino, A., Babazadeh, M., Pautasso, C.: Mashup development with web liquid streams. In: Daniel, F., Pautasso, C. (eds.) RMC 2015, CCIS 591, pp. 98–117. Springer, Heidelberg (2015)
5. Nouri, A., Daniel, F.: Interactive, live mashup development through UI-oriented computing. In: Daniel, F., Pautasso, C. (eds.) RMC 2015, CCIS 591, pp. 31–49. Springer, Heidelberg (2015)
6. Krug, M., Wiedemann, F., Gaedke, M.: SmartComposition: extending web applications to multi-screen mashups. In: Daniel, F., Pautasso, C. (eds.) RMC 2015, CCIS 591, pp. 50–62. Springer, Heidelberg (2015)
7. Díaz, O., Aldalur, I.A., Arellano, C., Medina, H., Firmenich, S.: Web mashups with WebMakeup. In: Daniel, F., Pautasso, C. (eds.) RMC 2015, CCIS 591, pp. 82–97. Springer, Heidelberg (2015)

Author Index

Printed in the United States
By Bookmasters